Julia Ward Howe

Later Lyrics

Julia Ward Howe

Later Lyrics

ISBN/EAN: 9783744796316

Printed in Europe, USA, Canada, Australia, Japan

Cover: Foto ©Thomas Meinert / pixelio.de

More available books at **www.hansebooks.com**

LATER LYRICS.

BY

JULIA WARD HOWE.

BOSTON:
J. E. TILTON & COMPANY.
1866.

Entered, according to Act of Congress, in the year 1865, by
J. E. TILTON & COMPANY,
In the Clerk's Office of the District Court of the District of Massachusetts.

Stereotyped by C. J. PETERS & SON, No. 13, Washington Street.

Press of GEO. C. RAND & AVERY, No. 3, Cornhill.

CONTENTS.

POEMS OF THE WAR.

	PAGE
OUR COUNTRY	9
THE FIRST MARTYR	12
APRIL 19	15
OUR ORDERS	18
REQUITAL	20
THE QUESTION	22
THE FLAG	24
HARVARD STUDENT'S SONG	29
ONE AND MANY	31
LEFT BEHIND	32
HYMN FOR A SPRING FESTIVAL, MAY 27, 1862	33
THE JEWELLER'S SHOP IN WAR-TIME	36
THE BATTLE-EUCHARIST	39
BATTLE-HYMN OF THE REPUBLIC	41

LYRICS OF THE STREET.

THE TELEGRAMS	45
THE WEDDING	49
THE FUNERAL	52
THE CHARITABLE VISITOR	55
THE FINE LADY	59
THE DARKENED HOUSE	62
THE OLD MAN'S WALK	64
AT A CORNER	66

iv   CONTENTS.

The Black Coach 67
Play 69
The Lost Jewel 71
Outside the Party 73
The Soul-Hunter 76
Street Yarn 79

PARABLES.

I. 85
II. 87
III. 89
IV. 93

HER VERSES.—A LYRICAL ROMANCE.

The Legacy 99
Blushes 101
Wishes 103
Fears 105
Resolves 107
Studies 109
Latin 110
A Dream 113
Waking 116
The Summons 117
Waiting 119
The End 122

POEMS OF STUDY AND EXPERIENCE.

To the Critic 127
Philosophy 129
Kosmos 131
First Causes 133
The Christ 135
The Church 137
The Crucifix 140

CONTENTS.

KENYON'S LEGACY	142
TO ONE WHO LIES IN FLORENCE	146
THE PRICE OF THE DIVINA COMMEDIA	149
A NEW SCULPTOR	152
A VICTIM OF TIBERIUS	156
CAIUS CÆSAR	160
CLAUDIUS	166
THE VISION OF PAUL	169
THE GOOD GUALDERALDA	172
1830 AND 1853	175
PERUGIA	181
OF WOMAN	186
AMANDA'S INVENTORY	190
LYKE-WAKE	192
BARGAINS	193
ROUGE GAGNE	195
THE TEA-PARTY	197
MAID AND MISTRESS	199
THE MODERATE MAN	203
WARNING	205
CONTRASTS	206
A VISION OF PALM SUNDAY	208
JEALOUSY	214
WITHOUT AND WITHIN	216
THE VOICE OF THE CATARACT	219
THE EVENING RIDE	221
NIGHT-MUSINGS	223
SUMMER NIGHT	226
EROS HAS WARNING	228
EROS DEPARTS	231
SIMPLE TALES.—I.	235
II.	240
THE ROSE IN THE JOURNAL	242
A DREAM OF DISTANCE	244
FAME AND FRIENDSHIP	246

CONTENTS.

A Woman's Prayer	248
The Last Bird	250
Farewell to Havana	253
A Wild Night	255
Baby's Shoes	258
Mother's Nonsense	261
The Babe's Lesson	263
"Servant to a Wooden Cradle"	266
The Unwelcome Message	269
My Crucifix	272
A Winter Thought	273
Spring-Blossoms	274
Remembrance	276
Little One	278
Chopin	281
Hamlet at the Boston	283
In my Valley	288
Endeavor	291
Meditation. — I.	293
II.	296
The House of Rest	299
A Visit to C. H.	303
A Leaf from the Bryant Chaplet	306
Henry Wilson's Silver Wedding	311
The New Exodus	313
Parricide	317
Pardon	322
Welcome	324

POEMS OF THE WAR.

POEMS OF THE WAR.

OUR COUNTRY.

On primal rocks she wrote her name,
Her towers were reared on holy graves,
The golden seed that bore her came
Swift-winged with prayer o'er ocean waves.

The Forest bowed his solemn crest,
And open flung his sylvan doors;
Meek Rivers led the appointed Guest
To clasp the wide-embracing shores;

Till, fold by fold, the broidered Land
To swell her virgin vestments grew,
While Sages, strong in heart and hand,
Her virtue's fiery girdle drew.

O Exile of the wrath of Kings!
O Pilgrim Ark of Liberty!
The refuge of divinest things,
Their record must abide in thee.

First in the glories of thy front
Let the crown jewel Truth be found;
Thy right hand fling with generous wont
Love's happy chain to furthest bound.

Let Justice with the faultless scales
Hold fast the worship of thy sons,
Thy commerce spread her shining sails
Where no dark tide of rapine runs.

So link thy ways to those of God,
So follow firm the heavenly laws,
That stars may greet thee, warrior-browed,
And storm-sped angels hail thy cause.

O Land, the measure of our prayers,
Hope of the world, in grief and wrong!
Be thine the blessing of the years,
The gift of faith, the crown of song.

THE FIRST MARTYR.

My five-years' darling, on my knee,
Chattered and toyed and laughed with me:
" Now tell me, mother mine," quoth she,
　" Where you went i' the afternoon."
" Alas! my pretty little life,
I went to see a sorrowing wife,
　Who will be widowed soon."

" Now, mother, what is that?" she said,
With wondering eyes and restless head:
" Will, then, her husband soon be dead?
　Tell me, why must he die?
Is he like flowers the frost doth sear,
Or like the birds, that, every year,
　Melt back into the sky?"

" No, love: the flowers may bloom their time,
The birdlings sing their merry chime,
Till bids them seek another clime

The Winter sharp and cold ;
But he who waits with fettered limb,
Nor God nor Nature sends for him, —
　　He is not weak nor old.

" He lies upon a prison bed
With sabre gashes on his head ;
And one short month will see him led
　　Where Vengeance wields the sword.
Then shall his form be lifted high,
And strangled in the public eye
　　With horrible accord."

" But, mother, say, what has he done?
Has he not robbed or murdered one?"
" My darling, he has injured none.
　　To free the wretched slaves
He led a band of chosen men,
Brave, but too few ; made captives then,
　　And doomed to felon graves."

" O mother ! let us go this day
To that sad prison, far away ;
The cruel governor we'll pray

To unloose the door so stout.
Some comfort we can bring him, sure:
And is he locked up so secure,
    We could not get him out?"

"No, darling: he is closely kept."
Then nearer to my heart she crept,
And, hiding there her beauty, wept
    For human misery.
Child! it is fit that thou shouldst weep;
The very babe unborn would leap
    To rescue such as he.

O babe unborn! O future race!
Heir of our glory and disgrace,
We cannot see thy veilèd face;
    But shouldst thou keep our crime,
No new Apocalypse need say
In what wild woe shall pass away
    The falsehood of the time.

APRIL 19.

A SPASM o'er my heart
 Sweeps like a burning flood;
A sentence rings upon mine ears,
 Avenge the guiltless blood!

Sit not in health and ease,
 Nor reckon loss nor gain,
When men who bear our country's flag
 Are set upon and slain,

Not by mistaken hearts
 With long oppression wrung,
Filled with great thoughts that ripen late,
 And madden, when they're young.

The murderer's wicked lust
   Their righteous steps withstood;
The zeal that thieves and pirates know
   Brought down the guiltless blood.

From every vein of mine
   Its fiery burthen take;
From every drop the burning coin
   Of righteous vengeance make.

Low let the city lie
   That thus her guests receives;
A smoking ruin to the eye
   Be marble walls and caves!

Thou God of love and wrath,
   That watchest on the wing,
Remorseless at those caitiff hearts
   Thy bolts of judgment fling!

APRIL 19.

Blot from the sight of heaven
　The city, where she stood,
And with thy might, avenging Right,
　Wipe out the guiltless blood!

OUR ORDERS.

Weave no more silks, ye Lyons looms,
    To deck our girls for gay delights!
The crimson flower of battle blooms,
    And solemn marches fill the night.

Weave but the flag whose bars to-day
    Drooped heavy o'er our early dead,
And homely garments, coarse and gray,
    For orphans that must earn their bread!

Keep back your tunes, ye viols sweet,
    That poured delight from other lands!
Rouse there the dancer's restless feet:
    The trumpet leads our warrior bands.

And ye that wage the war of words
  With mystic fame and subtle power,
Go, chatter to the idle birds,
  Or teach the lesson of the hour!

Ye Sibyl Arts, in one stern knot
  Be all your offices combined!
Stand close, while Courage draws the lot,
  The destiny of human kind.

And if that destiny could fail,
  The sun should darken in the sky,
The eternal bloom of Nature pale,
  And God, and Truth, and Freedom die!

REQUITAL.

He died beneath the uplifted thong
　Who spared for us a thousand lives :
He came to sing glad Israel's song ;
　We gave him Babylonian gyves.

With swelling heart and simple thought
　He warned us of the unheeded snare
Our chiefs discovered : vilely caught,
　They flung him back to perish there.

Did Pilate seal the Saviour's fate
　As still the shuddering Nations say,
When, in that hour of high debate,
　With ill-washed hands he turned away?

Sweet Christ, with flagellations brought
    To thine immortal martyrdom,
Cancel the bitter treasons wrought
    By men who bid thy kingdom come.

Their sinful blood we may not urge
    While Mercy stays thy righteous hand;
But take all ours, if that should purge
    The wicked patience of the land.

THE QUESTION.

Tell me, Master, am I free?
From the prison land I come,
From a mocked humanity,
From the fable of a home;

From the shambles, where my wife
With my baby at her breast,
Faded from my narrow life,
Rudely bartered, ill-possest.

Will you keep me, for my faith,
From the hound that scents my track,
From the riotous, drunken breath,
From the murder at my back?

Masters, ye are fighting long;
Well your trumpet-blast we know;
Are ye come to right a wrong?
Do we call you friend or foe?

God must come, for whom we pray,
Knowing his deliverance true;
Shall our men be left to say
He must work it free of you?

Fetters of a burning chain
Held the spirit of our braves;
Waiting for the nobler strain,
Silence told him *we* were slaves.

THE FLAG.

There's a flag hangs over my threshold, whose folds are more dear to me
Than the blood that thrills in my bosom its earnest of liberty;
And dear are the stars it harbors in its sunny field of blue
As the hope of a further heaven, that lights all our dim lives through.

But now should my guests be merry, the house is in holiday guise,
Looking out through its burnished windows like a score of welcoming eyes.
Come hither, my brothers, who wander in saintliness and in sin;
Come hither, ye pilgrims of Nature, my heart doth invite you in.

My wine is not of the choicest, yet bears it an honest
    brand;
And the bread that I bid you lighten, I break with no
    sparing hand:
But pause, ere ye pass to taste it, one act must
    accomplished be, —
Salute the flag in its virtue, before ye sit down with
    me.

The flag of our stately battles, not struggles of wrath
    and greed,
Its stripes were a holy lesson, its spangles a deathless
    creed:
'Twas red with the blood of freemen, and white with
    the fear of the foe;
And the stars that fight in their courses 'gainst tyrants
    its symbols know.

Come hither, thou son of my mother; we were reared
    in the self-same arms;
Thou hast many a pleasant gesture, thy mind hath its
    gifts and charms;

But my heart is as stern to question as mine eyes are
of sorrows full:
Salute the flag in its virtue, or pass on where others
rule!

Thou lord of a thousand acres, with heaps of uncounted gold,
The steeds of thy stall are haughty, thy lackeys cunning and bold:
I envy no jot of thy splendor, I rail at thy follies none, —
Salute the flag in its virtue, or leave my poor house alone!

Fair lady with silken flouncings, high waving thy stainless plume,
We welcome thee to our banquet, a flower of costliest bloom.
Let an hundred maids live widowed to furnish thy bridal bed;
But pause where the flag doth question, and bend thy triumphant head.

THE FLAG.

Take down now your flaunting banner; for a scout
  comes breathless and pale,
With the terror of death upon him; of failure is all
  his tale:
"They have fled while the flag waved o'er them,
  they've turned to the foe their back;
They are scattered, pursued, and slaughtered; the
  fields are all rout and wrack."

Pass hence then, the friends I gathered, a goodly
  company,
All ye that have manhood in you, go, perish for
  Liberty!
But I and the babes God gave me will wait with
  uplifted hearts,
With the firm smile ready to kindle, and the will to
  perform our parts.

When the last true heart lies bloodless, when the
  fierce and the false have won,
I'll press in turn to my bosom each daughter and
  either son:

Bid them loose the flag from its bearings, and we'll lay
 us down to rest
With the glory of home about us, and its freedom
 locked in our breast.

HARVARD STUDENT'S SONG.

REMEMBER ye the fateful gun that sounded
To Sumter's walls from Charleston's treacherous
  shore?
Remember ye how hearts indignant bounded
When our first dead came back from Baltimore?
The banner fell that every breeze had flattered,
The hum of thrift was hushed with sudden woe;
We raised anew the emblems shamed and shattered,
And turned a front resolved to meet the foe.

Remember ye how, out of boyhood leaping,
Our gallant mates stood ready for the fray,
As new-fledged eaglets rise, with sudden sweeping,
And meet unscared the dazzling front of day?
Our classic toil became inglorious leisure,
We praised the calm Horatian ode no more,
But answered back with song the martial measure,
That held its throb above the cannon's roar.

Remember ye the pageants dim and solemn,
Where Love and Grief have borne the funeral pall?
The joyless marching of the mustered column,
With arms reversed, to Him who conquers all?
Oh! give them back, thou bloody breast of Treason,
They were our own, the darlings of our hearts:
They come benumbed and frosted out of season,
With whom the summer of our youth departs.

Look back no more! our time has come, my brothers!
In Fate's high roll our names are written too:
We fill the mournful gaps left bare by others,
The ranks where Fear has never broken through.
Look, ancient Walls, upon our stern election!
Keep, Echoes dear, remembrance of our breath!
And gentle eyes, and hearts of pure affection,
Light us resolved to victory or death!

ONE AND MANY.

HE is dead with whom we spake;
Ere the latest war cloud brake,
Vanished, with the smile he wore
When we parted evermore.

As a star that leaves its place
Fills the heavens with passing grace,
Did he set our hearts aglow,
Loving loath to see him go.

Where he was, a shadow rests,
Veiling void in aching breasts:
He but heeds the immortal rule,
Lifted to the Beautiful!

LEFT BEHIND.

The foe is retreating, the field is clear;
My thoughts fly like lightning, my steps stay here;
I'm bleeding to faintness, no help is near:
    What, ho! comrades; what, ho!

The battle was deadly, the shots fell thick;
We leaped from our trenches, and charged them quick;
I knew not my wound till my heart grew sick:
    So there, comrades; so there.

We charged the left column, that broke and fled;
Poured powder for powder, and lead for lead:
So they must surrender, what matter who's dead?
    Who cares, comrades? who cares?

My soul rises up on the wings of the slain,
A triumph thrills through me that quiets the pain:
If it were yet to do, I would do it again!
    Farewell, comrades, farewell!

HYMN FOR A SPRING FESTIVAL,
MAY 27, 1862.

In this glad time of Spring
Nature doth garlands bring,
    Crowning her joys.
All that was seared with frost,
Buried, and mourned for lost,
With a new Pentecost,
    Flame-touched, doth rise.

Come, then, ye sons of men!
Stand, and take heart again,
    Blessing the year.
Earth fills her breast with food;
Odors enchant the wood;
Each leafy solitude
    Music doth cheer.

Where the war-trumpets blow,
Our legions meet the foe
   With deathful din;
But hosts unseen are there,
Fight and fatigue to share:
So we but strive with prayer,
   Steadfast, we win.

O hearts that wonder long!
O Truth that sufferest wrong!
   Meet in your might;
Lift the pure banner high;
Raise one impassioned cry,
Nobler than victory,—
   "God speed the right!"

Through the dark years of crime,
For this appointed time
   Justice did wait.
Purpose and Hope, that lay
Passive and dumb as clay,
Stand, in God's chosen day,
   Stronger than Fate.

We then, with faith increased,
Hold our fraternal feast,
    Death making sign,
Solemn as when he stood
Where our Supremest Good
Bade memory count his blood
    Dearer than wine.

All glories, Lord! are thine;
All joys are throbs divine
    Pulsed from thy breast.
As thine infinity,
Peace-crowned, returns to thee,
Let our toil gathered be
    Into thy rest.

THE JEWELLER'S SHOP IN WAR-TIME.

Past these counters wilt thou lead me,
Notes of luxury to read me
In the pearly shows and golden
That to outward boast embolden?
Watchful sit the shapes of sorrow.
Say: the Black Death comes to-morrow.

Bride, the altar-gifts are waiting
The permission of thy mating;
Heart and purse make brief unclasping
From the daily miser-grasping.
Fill the cup! away with sorrow!
Will the Black Death come to-morrow?

Lo! he lies in bloody heather,
'Neath the burning summer weather:
Not a drop his dry lip wetteth;
Dryer yet his sad eye setteth.

Rend thy bridal robes for sorrow:
Doth the Black Death wait the morrow?

See! the silver vessels goodly
Hands of hirelings stir not rudely;
Gems that deck the board's white wearing,
In a house of noble bearing;
Legendary urns of sorrow:
Death attends the feast to-morrow!

See! the rings of wild desire, —
Dreamy opal; diamond fire;
Emerald, green as summer grasses
Lit of sun that never passes;
Jets, the dim delights of sorrow,
That the Black Death buys, the morrow.

Chalice see and salver ghostly
That affright the gazer mostly;
Stirrup-cup that awes and blesses,
Cordial drop of last distresses;
Pearl of hope dissolved in sorrow,
Dear where Death is due the morrow.

Take me rather when the hours
Write their journal fair in flowers;
Where our sweet joys die and darken
With the firmament to hearken.
Soft in silence sinks our sorrow;
Resurrection comes to-morrow.

Life ye tear to shred and flitter,
Joying in the costly glitter
To rehearse each art-abortion
That consumes a widow's portion.
Lavish feast makes secret sorrow;
Pinch at heart brings Death to-morrow!

Take me where sweet doctrine, hoarded,
Stays the ravage, ill-afforded;
Wisdom's store, divinely pleasured,
Hero heart-beat, poet-measured.
Song that lightens out of sorrow
Shields from every Death to-morrow.

THE BATTLE-EUCHARIST.

ABOVE the seas of gold and glass
The Christ, transfigured, stands to-day;
Below, in troubled currents, pass
The tidal fates of man away.

Through that environed blessedness
Our sorrow cannot wholly rise,
Nor his swift sympathy redress
The anguish that in Nature lies.

Yet mindful from his banquet sends
The guest of God a cup of wine,
And shares a morsel with his friends,
Who, wondering, wait without the shrine.

Remain with us, O Lord! remain;
Our faint souls will not let thee go:
Bear with us this surpassing pain,
Abide our sacrament of woe,

While ghostly hands from battle-fields
Reproach with succor long delayed,
And all the wealth our treasure yields
Buys not the power to hasten aid.

O Christ, that multipliest bread!
Thou Feeder of the multitude,
On them thy heart's redemption shed,
Feed our beloved with heavenly food;

And open wide the gates of thought,
That, sitting at this feast divine,
Our faith may see deliverance wrought
By pangs that bear the mark of thine.

BATTLE-HYMN OF THE REPUBLIC.

MINE eyes have seen the glory of the coming of the
Lord:
He is trampling out the vintage where the grapes of
wrath are stored;
He hath loosed the fateful lightning of his terrible
swift sword:
    His truth is marching on.

I have seen Him in the watch-fires of a hundred
circling camps;
They have builded Him an altar in the evening dews
and damps;
I can read His righteous sentence by the dim and
flaring lamps.
    His day is marching on.

I have read a fiery gospel, writ in burnished rows of steel:
"As ye deal with my contemners, so with you my grace shall deal;
Let the Hero, born of woman, crush the serpent with his heel,
 Since God is marching on."

He has sounded forth the trumpet that shall never call retreat;
He is sifting out the hearts of men before his judgment-seat:
Oh! be swift, my soul, to answer Him! be jubilant, my feet!
 Our God is marching on.

In the beauty of the lilies Christ was born across the sea,
With a glory in his bosom that transfigures you and me:
As he died to make men holy, let us die to make men free,
 While God is marching on.

LYRICS OF THE STREET.

THE TELEGRAMS.

BRING the hearse to the station,
   When one shall demand it, late ;
For that dark consummation
   The traveller must not wait.
Men say not by what connivance
   He slid from his weight of woe,
Whether sickness or weak contrivance,
   But we know him glad to go.
        On and on and ever on !
        What next?

Nor let the priest be wanting
   With his hollow eyes of prayer,
While the sexton wrenches, panting,
   The stone from the dismal stair.

But call not the friends who left him
    When fortune and pleasure fled :
Mortality hath not bereft him,
    That they should confront him, dead.
        On and on and ever on !
            What next?

Bid my mother be ready :
    We are coming home to-night :
Let my chamber be still and shady
    With the softened nuptial light.
We have travelled so gayly, madly,
    No shadow hath crossed our way ;
Yet we come back like children, gladly,
    Joy-spent with our holiday.
        On and on and ever on !
            What next?

Stop the train at the landing,
    And search every carriage through ;
Let no one escape your handing,
    None shiver, or shrink from view.

Three blood-stained guests expect him;
Three murders oppress his soul;
Be strained every nerve to detect him
Who feasted, and killed, and stole.
On and on and ever on!
What next?

Be rid of the notes they scattered;
The great house is down at last;
The image of gold is shattered,
And never can be recast.
The bankrupts show leaden features,
And weary, distracted looks,
While harpy-eyed, wolf-souled creatures
Pry through their dishonored books.
On and on and ever on!
What next?

Let him hasten, lest worse befall him,
To look on me, ere I die:
I will whisper one curse to appall him,
Ere the black flood carry me by.

His bridal? The friends forbid it;
   I have shown them his proofs of guilt;
Let him hear, with my laugh, who did it;
   Then hurry, Death, as thou wilt!
       On and on and ever on!
          What next?

Thus the living and dying daily
   Flash forward their wants and words,
While still on Thought's slender railway
   Sit scathless the little birds:
They heed not the sentence dire
   By magical hands exprest,
And only the sun's warm fire
   Stirs softly their happy breast.
       On and on and ever on!
          God next!

THE WEDDING.

IN her satin gown so fine
Trips the bride within the shrine.
Waits the street to see her pass,
Like a vision in a glass.
Roses crown her peerless head :
Keep your lilies for the dead !

Something of the light without
Enters with her, veiled about ;
Sunbeams, hiding in her hair,
Please themselves with silken wear ;
Shadows point to what shall be
In the dim futurity.

Wreathe with flowers the weighty yoke
Might of mortal never broke.
From the altar of her vows
To the grave's unsightly house
Measured is the path, and made:
All the work is planned and paid.

As a girl, with ready smile,
Where shall rise some ponderous pile,
On the chosen, festal day,
Turns the initial sod away,
So the bride with fingers frail
Founds a temple or a jail, —

Or a palace, it may be,
Flooded full with luxury,
Open yet to deadliest things,
And the Midnight Angel's wings.
Keep its chambers purged with prayer:
Faith can guard it, Love is rare.

Organ, sound thy wedding-tunes!
Priest, recite the sacred runes!
Hast no ghostly help nor art
Can enrich a selfish heart,
Blessing bind 'twixt greed and gold,
Joy with bloom for bargain sold?

Hail, the wedded task of life!
Mending husband, moulding wife.
Hope brings labor, labor peace;
Wisdom ripens, goods increase;
Triumph crowns the sainted head,
And our lilies wait the dead.

THE FUNERAL.

As I passed down the street,
   Sighing and singing,
Making its pavement sweet
   With flowery flinging,
Came the unwelcome feet,
   Sad burthen bringing.

Death! I forgot thou shouldst
   Harvest this morning:
Not for thy festival
   Was my adorning;
Yet to my heart I take,
   Duteous, thy warning.

Out of the pleasant day
    Darkly they lay thee :
Shall thine accustomed haunts
    No more display thee ;
Shall thy high house of life
    Cease to obey thee.

Done are thy deeds of good,
    And thy malefeasance ;
Ended the years of dole,
    And the short pleasance :
Thou art a power no more,
    Only a presence.

Hot tears bedim the eyes
    That would behold thee ;
Death-spasms wring the hearts
    Whose loves infold thee ;
While monumental Grief
    Waits to inmould thee.

Whither, ah! whither gone,
　From our wild weeping?
For what new threshing-floor
　Bound with strange reaping?
Taken, we know no more,
　Into God's keeping.

THE CHARITABLE VISITOR.

She carries no flag of fashion, her clothes are but
 passing plain,
Though she comes from a city palace all jubilant with
 her reign :
She threads a bewildering alley, with ashes and dust
 thrown out,
And fighting and cursing children, who mock as she
 moves about.

Why walk you this way, my lady, in the snow and
 slippery ice?
These are not the shrines of virtue, — here misery
 lives, and vice :
Rum helps the heart of starvation to a courage bold
 and bad ;
And women are loud and brawling, while men sit
 maudlin and mad.

I see in the corner yonder the boy with a broken
   arm,
And the mother whose blind wrath did it, — strange
   guardian from childish harm!
That face will grow bright at your coming, but your
   steward might come as well,
Or better the Sunday teacher that helped him to read
   and spell.

Oh! I do not come of my willing, with froward and
   restless feet:
I have pleasant tasks in my chamber, and friends well-
   beloved to greet.
To follow the dear Lord Jesus, I walk in the storm
   and snow;
Where I find the trace of his footsteps, there lilies and
   roses grow.

He said that to give was blessèd, more blessèd than
   to receive;
But what could he take, dear angels, of all that we
   had to give,

Save a little pause of attention, and a little thrill of
    delight,
When the dead were waked from their slumbers, and
    the blind recalled to sight?

Say, the King came forth with the morning, and opened
    his palace doors,
Thence flinging his gifts like sunbeams that break upon
    marble floors;
But the wind with wild pinions caught them, and
    carried them round about:
Though I looked till mine eyes were dazzled, I never
    could make them out.

But he bade me go far and find them, "go seek them
    with zeal and pain:
The hand is most welcome to me that brings me mine
    own again;
And those who follow them furthest, with faithful
    searching and sight,
Are brought with joy to my presence, and sit at my
    feet all night."

So, hither and thither walking, I gather them broadly
    cast;
Where yonder young face doth sicken, it may be the
    best and last.
In no void or vague of duty I come to his aid to-day:
I bring God's love to his bedside, and carry God's
    gift away.

THE FINE LADY.

HER heart is set on folly,
    An amber gathering straws:
She courts each poor occurrence,
    Heeds not the heavenly laws.
            Pity her!

She has a little beauty,
    And she flaunts it in the day,
While the selfish wrinkles, spreading,
    Steal all its charm away.
            Pity her!

She has a little money,
    And she flings it everywhere:
'Tis a gewgaw on her bosom,
    A tinsel in her hair.
            Pity her!

She has a little feeling,
　She spreads a foolish net
That snares her own weak footsteps,
　Not his for whom 'tis set.
　　　　　　　Pity her!

Ye harmless household drudges,
　Your draggled daily wear
And horny palms of labor
　A softer heart may bear.
　　　　　　　Pity her!

Ye steadfast ones, whose burthens
　Weigh valorous shoulders down,
With hands that cannot idle,
　And brows that will not frown,
　　　　　　　Pity her!

Ye saints, whose thoughts are folded
　As graciously to rest
As a dove's stainless pinions
　Upon her guileless breast,
　　　　　　　Pity her!

But most, ye helpful angels
That send distress and work,
Hot task and sweating forehead,
To heal man's idle irk,
    Pity her!

THE DARKENED HOUSE.

ONE year ago this dreary night,
    This house, that in my way
Checks the swift pulses of delight,
    Was cordial glad, and gay.

The household angels tended there
    Their ivy-cinctured bower,
And by the hardier plant grew fair
    A lovely lily-flower.

The skies rained sunshine on its head,
    It throve in summer air:
"How straight and sound!" the father said;
    The mother said, "How fair!"

One little year is gathering up
  Its glories to depart;
The skies have left one marble drop
  Within the lily's heart.

For growth and bloom no more avails
  The Seasons' changing breath:
Fixed in sad constancy, it feels
  The sculpture-touch of Death.

But from its breast let golden rays,
  Immortal, break and rise,
Linking the sorrow-clouded days
  With dawning paradise.

THE OLD MAN'S WALK.

Into the sadness of the winter night
    I bear my heart:
Shunning the crowded streets, the glaring light,
    I walk apart.

With trembling feet and head astound I go,
    With cheeks chill-wet:
I must return unto that house of woe;
    I cannot yet.

Unhappy words compel me from the hearth
    Of love bereft;
Should send me reckless o'er the rolling earth,
    With bosom cleft.

THE OLD MAN'S WALK.

O Stranger! ask not why I stray abroad
    Thus out of time.
Mine eye has not the furtive glance of fraud,
    The leer of crime.

Deep Night, within thy gloomy catafalque
    Bury my grief;
And, while thy candles light my funeral walk,
    Promise relief.

Let lightsome spirits that outwatch thy reign,
    Dawn's sentinels,
Shed golden balsam for the sons of pain
    In prison cells.

"Ave," I hear the pitying angels say;
    From depths they call;
"Through all Grief's multitude Heaven makes a
    way."
    Heaven rest us all!

AT A CORNER.

Here should I meet you, here only, recalling
The soul-drunken look you vouchsafed me one day,
That, like a spark in some hidden mine falling,
Shook my frail senses, and swept me away.

What did that look portend? dark was its meaning,
Faded in tears the swift gleam of delight;
Ask the deep thoughts of eternity's screening,
Ask the wide stars in the bosom of night.

Like some winged Seraphim, never descending,
That for a moment unveils to our view:
Sudden its ravishment, bitter its ending;
Love flashed a promise that Life never knew.

THE BLACK COACH.

In the black coach you must ride,—
You, so dainty once a time.
We who saw your bloom of pride,
Stifle now the crop of crime,
Lest its poisonous, fruitful birth
Scatter monsters o'er the earth.

She had holidays as gay
As the highest you have known,
Lady, flitting fast away,
With your chariot for a throne.
Wild-flowers for a moment please
In the hands of pampered ease.

Lifted, like a summer treasure
In a golden goblet placed,
To decline in mournful leisure,
Scorned, untended, and disgraced;
With the meadow yet in sight
Where the daisies glisten white.

Come, a carriage blacker still,
Narrowed to the form you bear;
Bring the last of good and ill;
Take the leavings of despair.
Death's cold purity condense
Vaporous sin to soul's intense.

Ere the prison-gates unswing,
Let the spirit portals ope;
While the Winter holds the Spring
Shall the grave-mound cover hope;
Come the pang that ends all woe,
God can better pardon so.

PLAY.

FROM yon den of double-dealing
    With its Devil's host,
Come I, maddened out of healing.
    All is lost.

So the false wine cannot blind me,
    Nor the braggart toast,
But I know that Hell doth bind me;
    All is lost.

Where the lavish gain attracts us,
    And the easy cost,
While the damning dicer backs us,
    All is lost.

Blest the rustic in his furrows,
        Toil and sweat-embossed;
Blest are honest souls in sorrows:
        All is lost.

Wifely love, the closer clinging
        When men need thee most,
Shall I come, dishonor bringing?
        All is lost.

Babe in silken cradle lying,
        To low music tossed,
Will they wake thee for my dying?
        All is lost.

Yonder, where the river grimly
        Whitens like a ghost,
Must I plunge and perish dimly:
        All is lost.

THE LOST JEWEL.

Cast on the turbid current of the street,
    My pearl doth swim;
Oh for the diver's cunning hands and feet
    To come to him!

No: I'll not seek the madness of thine eyes,
    Since, day by day,
Life brings its noiseless blessings from the skies;
    For which we pray.

While patient Duty, helped of heavenly Art,
    Her way pursues,
And holy loves re-edify the heart
    The passions use.

God's hand can bring unheard-of gifts to light
    From Fate's deep sea ;
Has pearls enough to recompense the right,
    Only not thee.

OUTSIDE THE PARTY.

THICK throng the snow-flakes, the evening is dreary,
Glad rings the music in yonder gay hall;
On her who listens here, friendless and weary,
Heavier chill than the winter's doth fall.

At yon clear window, light-opened before me,
Glances the face I have worshipped so well:
There's the fine gentleman, grand in his glory;
There, the fair smile by whose sweetness I fell.

This is akin to him, shunned and forsaken,
That at my bosom sobs low, without bread;
Had not such pleading my marble heart shaken,
I had been quiet, long since, with the dead.

Oh! could I enter there, ghastly and squalid,
Stand in men's eyes with my spirit o'erborne,
Show them where roses bloomed, crushed now and pallid,
What he found innocent, leaving forlorn, —

How the fair ladies would fail from their dances,
Trembling, aghast at my horrible tale!
How would he shrink from my words and my glances!
How would they shrink from him, swooning and pale!

This is the hair that was soft to enchain him;
Snakelike, it snarls on my beautiless brow:
These are the hands that were fond to detain him
With a sense-magic then, powerless now!

No: could I come, like a ghost, to affright him,
How should that heal my wound, silence my pain?
Had I the wrath of God's lightning to smite him,
That could not bring me my lost peace again.

Ne'er let him grieve while good fortunes betide him,
Ne'er count again the poor game lost of old;
When he comes forth, with his young bride beside him,
Here shall they find us both, dead in the cold.

THE SOUL-HUNTER.

Who hunts so late 'neath evening skies,
A smouldering love-brand in his eyes?
His locks outshame the black of night,
Its stars are duller than his sight
  Who hunts so late, so dark.

A drooping mantle shrouds his form,
To shield him from the winter's storm?
Or is there something at his side,
That, with himself, he strives to hide,
  Who hunts so late, so dark?

He hath such promise, silver sweet,
Such silken hands, such fiery feet,

That, where his look has charmed the prey,
His swift-winged passion forces way,
    Who hunts so late, so dark.

Sure no one underneath the moon
Can whisper to so soft a tune :
The hours would flit from dusk to dawn
Lighter than dews upon the lawn
    With him, so late, so dark.

But, should there break a day of need,
Those hands will try no valorous deed :
No help is in that sable crest,
Nor manhood in that hollow breast
    That sighed so late, so dark.

O maiden ! of the salt waves make
Thy sinless shroud, for God's dear sake ;
Or to the flame commit thy bloom ;
Or lock thee, living, in the tomb
    So desolate and dark, —

Before thou list one stolen word
Of him who lures thee like a bird.
He wanders with the Devil's bait,
For human souls he lies in wait,
    Who hunts so late, so dark.

STREET YARN.

Roses caged in windows, heighten
  Your faint blooms to-day;
Silks and sheeny satins, brighten;
  He has passed this way!

Could ye keep his fleeting presence
  Gone beyond recall,
But a little of his essence,
  I would have you all.

Arabesque so quaint and shady,
  That mightst catch his eye
To adorn a stately lady
  Ere her hour went by,

Canst assure me that his glancing
  Rested on thy fold?
Did that set your purples dancing?
  Wake the sleepy gold?

Ye neglected apple-venders
  Mouldering in the street,
Did he curse between your tenders,
  Spurning with his feet?

Then must I an alms deliver
  For his graceless pride;
Could I buy his sins forever,
  I'd not be denied.

Paying patiently his ransom
  Never conscience-pricked;
Cheating Justice of her handsome
  Heartless derelict.

Did he view thee, ancient steeple,
   With thy weird clock-face,
Frowning down on sinful people
   Passing out of grace?

Nay, respond not to my question
   With thy prate of time :
Things to which my soul must hasten
   Lie beyond thy chime.

With no circumstance to screen us,
   We must meet again :
I shall bid God judge between us,
   Answering Amen.

PARABLES.

PARABLES.

I.

"I SENT a child of mine to-day;
   I hope you used him well."
"Now, Lord, no visitor of yours
   Has waited at my bell.

The children of the Millionnaire
   Run up and down our street;
I glory in their well-combed hair,
   Their dress and trim complete.

But yours would in a chariot come
   With thorough-breds so gay;
And little merry maids and men
   To cheer him on his way."

"Stood, then, no child before your door?"
  The Lord, persistent, said.
" Only a ragged beggar-boy,
  With rough and frowzy head.

The dirt was crusted on his skin,
  His muddy feet were bare;
The cook gave victuals from within;
  I cursed his coming there."

What sorrow, silvered with a smile,
  Slides o'er the face divine?
What tenderest whisper thrills rebuke?
  " The beggar-boy was mine!"

II.

ONCE, where men of high pretension
    For the Lord did wait,
Suffer did their pride declension;
    Angry grew their state.

One, impatient, snaps his fingers;
    One torments his hair;
One, albeit no pride of singers,
    Hums a broken air.

Sitting low apart, a modest
    Maiden waited too;
Little weary one, thou ploddest
    Ill thy week's work through!

Comes the Lord. From long abiding
    They uprise in haste;
With their greeting mingles chiding
    For the time they waste.

"Lord, I am a merchant wealthy;
   Commerce holds me dear;
Competition enters stealthy
   While I tarry here."

"Lord, for me recondite dinners
   Chill on festive boards;
Waste the games, and haste the winners,
   While I wait thy words."

To this folly of upbraiding
   Says the Master, "Yes:
You have waited too, my maiden;
   Seek you not redress?"

"Waiting is such holy pleasure
   For a joy most dear;
I had rapture out of measure,
   Knowing thou wert near."

III.

BESIDE this goodly mansion's gate
    I'll pause, and rest a while:
Its master will not have me wait;
    He beckons with a smile.
" Now, friend, what might your errand be?
Will you walk in for charity?"

Thus I returned him: " Could you know
    The treasures in my pack,
And all the bravery and show
    I carry at my back,
The merchant's pains you should requite,
Not shame him with the beggar's mite."

" If it content you, open out
    The goods you praise so well."
" I've turned the rolling earth about
    For that which here I sell;
No trumpery for the servants' hall:
I only heed the master's call.

Behold these painful broideries rare,
    The costliest Fashion knows ;
Such as the chief Sultanas wear,
    Steeped with the attar rose."
" Your shawl is faded, patched, and poor :
It pleases not ; show something more."

" This crystal phial, art-embossed,
    A balsam doth contain
For whose delight an empire's cost
    Were scarcely spent in vain."
" It cannot match one clover-bloom :
Bring other business, — pass perfume."

" Behold this weighty carcanet,
    Whose links of sullen gold
Would seem to bind the Favorite yet
    In Love's triumphant hold."
" The iron rusts through these gilded chains,
As smiles discover torture-pains."

"Last, then, this diamond, with a light
    Kindled 'neath tropic skies :
A slave toiled twenty years of night,
    Bleeding, to win this prize."
"One impulse of the blood you name
Would put your Kohinoor to shame."

"Shall your encounter make me poor,
    And desolate of bread?
If all my wealth beside your door
    Buys not a pilgrim's bed,
At the next inn I'll set me down,
And travel to the market-town."

"Friend!" said the Master, "coming here,
    You passed an unseen bound ;
And in the outer region drear
    No hostelry is found.
I question all who pass this way,
And grant them leave to go or stay.

But in my mansion, too, is wealth
    Of garments glad and white :
My chains are helpful bonds of health ;
    My jewels, heart's delight ;
My perfumes waste no joy divine :
Enter ; for all I have is thine.

IV.

Lord of life, why must thou seek me
    In this desert wild?
Why so tenderly bespeak me,
    Fallen and sin-defiled?

Should thy feet, so fair and glorious,
    That in heaven's ways go,
Tread the stony paths laborious
    That the wicked know?

In abysses darkly yawning,
    Where the lost are pent,
Shouldst thou spread the purple awning
    Of thy sheltering tent?

See! the hell-flames gather round thee,
    Raging for thy life:
Tongues of thief and ribald wound thee
    Worse than spear or knife.

Oh! of all my deeds abhorrèd
   Is not this the worst,
Fronting thine anointed forehead
   With this woe accurst?

Angels, bear him without rudeness
   To the breath of morn,
Veiling with your crowns the voidness
   Where his brow is shorn.

Use no whisper of the evil
   That his hand hath done,
Lest a saint become a devil
   Torturing such an one.

And that wound, whose deadly feeling
   Makes the bosom faint,
Reconcile with swift annealing,
   Purge from mortal taint.

Call a feast of stately measure
  With a solemn joy,
With all courtesy and pleasure
  To him sitting by.

Gather up his long-lost kindred,
  Angered and estranged;
For each good gift bring an hundred,
  Since his heart is changed.

Bind the robe upon his shoulder,
  On his hand the ring;
Since, while Love is treasure-holder,
  Sorrow must be king.

HER VERSES: A LYRICAL ROMANCE.

THE LEGACY.

HER verses, — where she lies
The tall trees bend and whisper ;
Soft voices from the skies
Recall the tuneful lisper :
The sunny nooks she loved,
Her flower-beds untended,
Afflict us with neglect,
Like fair things ill-befriended.

Yet 'tis so merciful
That Time wipes out our traces,
And that the thick-set moss
Grows o'er our darkened faces,
Till but some faithful heart
Our faded traits comprises,
And sorrow, dead in earth,
In harmless beauty rises.

She had a guileless heart,
And Life was rude to grieve it;
She had a soul of fire,
And Heaven is kind to shrive it:
The years are past that said,
" Keep long this seal unbroken;
But, when my name's forgot,
Then let my words be spoken."

So, standing at her grave,
With trembling hands I gather
The blossoms of her life,
Bedimmed with rust and weather.
O World! while thus I wave
Her dead hand's blessing o'er thee,
Think 'tis my other self
Whose heart lies bare before thee.

BLUSHES.

I CANNOT make him know my love;
　　Nor from myself conceal
The pangs that rankle in my breast,
　　Sharper than flame or steel.

Could I but reach a hand to him,
　　My very finger's thrill
Would close, like tendrils, round the strength
　　Of his belovèd will.

Could I but lift mine eyes to his,
　　My glowing soul, unrolled,
Would flash like sunset on his sight,
　　In fiery red and gold.

Yet pause, my unflecked soul, and think
    How vexed Penelope
Forsook her nuptial joy, that love
    Should wait on modesty.

For gentle souls must keep their bounds,
    Nor rudely snatch at bliss:
The very sun should lose his light
    In giving it amiss.

So, when I die, cross tenderly
    My palms upon my breast,
And let some faithful hand compose
    My tired limbs to rest.

But thou shalt fold this kerchief white,
    And lay it on my face,
Saying, "She died of love untold;
    But she is dead in grace."

WISHES.

I would I might approach thee,
    As the moon draws near the cloud,
With still and stately courtesy,
    Clear-eyed and solemn-browed;
But, when their meeting comes, her face
    In his deep breast doth hide,
The heavens are still, in solemn joy,
    The world is glorified.

I would I might approach thee,
    As music, swift afloat,
Surprises, with its sudden joy,
    A wanderer in a boat:

The sordid walls of life fall down
    Before that clarion clear;
A passing rapture oft recalled
    When days grow blank and drear.

I would I might approach thee,
    As breezes fresh and pure,
Unsighted, breathe on fevered lips,
    And throbbing temples cure;
As Joy and Love, and healthful Hope,
    Visit some chosen heart,
And enter, softly welcomed there,
    And never more depart.

FEARS.

OH! how shall I grow fair enough
   For thee to look upon?
I am but the poor shallow water
   That glistens in the sun,
That darkens, mean and beautiless,
   When his brief glance moves on.

Oh! what shall raise me to thy sphere?
   How shall my thoughts aspire?
I am the string that warbles to
   A poet's touch of fire:
He flings it by, — how dumb and low
   Sinks the forgotten lyre!

Remember, then, my humble heart
   That trembled with surprise ;
Recall the faith that dared to meet
   The question of thine eyes :
Shall these not make me dear to thee
   Through Love's eternities?

RESOLVES.

You never knew how cruel kind
    Was the caress you gave ;
You never meant to light a flame
    Should smoulder in my grave.

From gentle studies, arts beloved,
    My thoughts all fix on thee ;
And Peace dissolves before my sight,
    And Duty cannot be.

Oh ! speak one word so kindly rude,
    So greatly stern and true,
That I may kiss thy feet for shame,
    And rise, absolved and new.

Then with some song of noblest worth
  I'll pay this truant rhyme,
And stretch my stolen broidery to
  The boundless tasks of Time.

STUDIES.

SLOWLY roll the wheels of Science
On the flowery ways of Love:
Clogged with sweets, the cheated pedant
Waits, forgetful of remove.

Or like Icarus aspiring
To the nearness of the sun;
See, the waxen wings are melted,
The ambitious race is run!

Love has neither past nor future
Till thou break its awful vow;
Neither was nor shall be blessèd:
It is one eternal Now.

LATIN.

HERE amid shadows, lovingly embracing,
Dropt from above by apple-trees unfruitful,
With a chance scholar, caught and held to help me,
  Read I in Horace;

Lost in the figures, lawless in the metrum,
Piecing the classic phrase with homespun English,
Bridging doubtful meanings with such daring fictions
  As move his wonder.

Dust lay condensed on the covers lexiconic, —
Tacitus above stairs, quasi sub-neglected,
Very little progress since I saw your godship,
  Day to be remembered!

Avè, sweet Horace, all thy wonder graces
(Soul of perfection, with a change of rainbows)
Less must delight me than thy fervent nature,
    Foremost in friendship.

" We with one bound will pursue the silent journey :
Ibimus, ibimus, — let one urn contain us ! "
Which would survive, to choke Love's glowing embers
    With Life's gray ashes?

Happy thy Mæcenas ! happier thou to praise him,
Twining thy best beauties round the brow thou lovest :
Oh ! to nobly name whom the deep heart doth worship
    Is a boon most holy.

Yonder by the high-road, from the post-town leading,
Cometh at seasons a worn and dusty carriage :
Two white bony horses, rudely loricated,
    Drag it behind them.

In the carriage mostly come my born relations,
Very keen to see me in the rural season;
Board and bedding gratis, compliments at parting:
    "Come again next summer."

Oh! if one I knew of hastened down the high-road,
Like a heaven-sent angel, present to petition,
Would I sit searching thy disjointed meanings,
    Horace the Dainty?

Should I not then fling far the well-bound volume,
Decent in sheep-skins thou wert never blest with?
For this heart of mine, high leaping, wild rejoicing,
    Then would be the poet.

A DREAM.

A WOMAN came, wearing a veil;
Her features were burning and pale;
At the door of the shrine doth she kneel,
And waileth out, bowing her head,
" Ye men of remembrance and dread,
Exorcise the pangs that I feel.

A boat that is torn with the tide,
A mountain with flame in its side
That rends its devouring way,
A feather the whirlwind lifts high,
Are not wilder or weaker than I,
Since Love makes my bosom his prey.

Ye Saints, I fall down at your feet;
Thou Virgin, so piteous to greet,
Reach hither the calm of your hands;
Ye statues of power and of art,
Let your marble weight lie on my heart,
Hold my madness with merciful bands."

The priest takes his candle and book
With the pity of scorn in his look,
And chants the dull Mass through his teeth;
But the penitent, clasping his knees,
Cries, " Vain as the sough of the breeze
Are thy words to the anguish of death."

The priest, with reproval and frown,
Bids the listless attendant reach down
The water that sprinkles from sin.
" Your water is water," she cries :
" The further its foolishness flies,
The fiercer the flames burn within."

"Get thee hence to the cell and the scourge!"
The priest in his anger doth urge,
"Or the fire of the stake thou shalt prove,
Maintaining with blasphemous tongue
That the mass-book and censer, high swung,
Cannot cast out the demon of Love."

Then the Highest stept down from his place,
While the depths of his wonderful face
The thrill of compassion did move:
"Come, hide thee," he cried, "in this breast;
I summon the weary to rest;
With love I exorcise thy love."

WAKING.

Soft as the touch of twilight that restores
The hard-bound earth from summer sweat and strain,
This dream of morning soothed my fevered soul,
And gave me to my gentleness again.

So, bathed in pearly sweets, I oped mine eyes,
And saw the beauty that the morning paints,
And saw the shadows strengthen in the sun
With the calm willingness of dying saints.

Oh! had I then to passion died, such peace
Had filled my parting as transfigures Death;
But thou didst turn me backward with a word,
And Love celestial fled Love's human breath.

THE SUMMONS.

I EXPECT you in September
With the glory of the year :
You shall make the Autumn precious,
And the death of Summer dear ;
You shall help the days that shorten,
With a lengthening of delight ;
You shall whisper long-drawn blisses
Through the gathering screen of night.

I will lead you. dream-enchanted,
Where the fairest grasses grow ;
I will hear your murmured music
Where the fresh winds pipe and blow.
On the brown heath, weird-encircled,
Shall our noiseless footsteps fall, —
We, communing with twin counsel.
Each to other all in all.

Leave the titles that men owe thee;
Like the first pair let us meet;
Name the world all over to me,
New-created at thy feet;
Gentle task and duteous learning,
I will hang upon thy breath
With the tender zeal of childhood,
With the constancy of death.

What shall be the gods declare not, —
They who stamp Love's burning coin
Into spangles of a moment,
Into stars that deathless shine.
Oh! the foolish music lingers;
For the theme is heavenly dear:
I expect you in September,
With the glories of the year.

WAITING.

I HAVE set my house in order
For a stately step to grace ;
I have bidden the mirrors keep record
Of a never-forgotten face ;
I have brightened with thrifty cunning
The walls of my sylvan home :
They are beautiful in the shadow
Of him who vouchsafes to come.

I have swept the leaves from the greensward,
And the gray stones twinkle and shine ;
I have loosened each fretful tangle
Of the twisted cedar and vine ;
I have ordered the waters waste not
Their splendors upon mine eye,
But to wait, like my heart, for thy footsteps,
And gush when thou drawest nigh.

Myself I would dress for thy presence;
But there I must stand and weep,
Since the years that teach Love's value
His vanishing treasure sweep.
But words that are spells of magic,
And merciful looks and ways,
Shall brighten the rusted features
That faded when none did praise.

Thou gracious and lordly creature,
Do the trees, when thou passest by,
Let down their fair arms to enlace thee,
And the flowers reach up to thine eye?
Do they wait, all athrill, when thou passest,
For a touch of thy life divine?
Do they fold their meek hands when thou fleetest,
And die for a breath of thine?

My heart has leapt forth to embrace thee;
It clings, like a babe, to thy breast;
And my blood is a storm-stirred ocean
That waits for the word of rest.

Time loses his paltry measure
Now that Love's eterne draws near,
And the lingering moments that part us
Are endless in hope and fear.

Oh! what if, beyond thy sunshine,
Some gathering storm should brood?
Thy rapture, forsaking, shall leave me
Alone with God's orphanhood.
The heart thou hast blest so inly
Shall wait no inglorious breath:
Come hither, then, ye who walk twinly;
So enter here, Love and Death!

THE END.

DEATH entered where Love was waiting
With the frosted lily-crown, —
Pale pontiff, shadow-mating,
Waving the life-flame down.

His slaves, with robes of whiteness,
Shrouded the glowing face :
Gone is the vision of brightness,
A ghost is in its place.

They bore her with solemn knelling,
By saintly crypt and nave,
To her new-appointed dwelling, —
The cloisters of the grave.

THE END.

There, 'mong the silent sisters,
She tarries, with folded palms :
Where the passing torch-light glisters,
They answer in whispered psalms.

But as one the convent hideth,
At the festivals of God,
From the covert where she bideth,
Sends holy song abroad ;

So she, whom then we buried
With manifold sob and strain,
Sends back her song, love-varied,
To waken our joy again, —

Sends back the flame of fervor
That warms not her frozen breast,
To guide Love's true deserver
To her place in the fields of rest.

POEMS OF STUDY AND EXPERIENCE.

TO THE CRITIC.

OF all my verses, say that one is good,
So shalt thou give more praise than Hope might claim;
And from my poet-grave, to vex thy soul,
No ghost shall rise, whose deeds demand a name.

A thousand loves, and only one shall stand
To show us what its counterfeits should be;
The blossoms of a spring-tide, and but one
Bears the world's fruit, — the seed of History.

A thousand rhymes shall pass, and only one
Show, crystal-shod, the Muse's twinkling feet;
A thousand pearls the haughty Ethiop spurned
Ere one could make her luxury complete.

In goodliest palaces, some meanest room
The owner's smallness shields contentedly.
Nay, further: of the manifold we are,
But one pin's point shall pass eternity.

Exalt, then, to the greatness of the throne
One only of these beggarlings of mine;
I with the rest will dwell in modest bounds:
The chosen one shall glorify the line.

PHILOSOPHY.

NAKED and poor thou goest, Philosophy!
Thy robe of serge hath lain beneath the stars;
Thy weight of tresses, ponderously free,
Of iron hue, no golden circlet bars.

Thy pale page, Study, by thy side doth hold,
As by Cyprigna's her persuasive boy:
Twin sacks thou bear'st; one doth thy gifts infold,
Whose modest tendering proves immortal joy.

The other at thy patient back doth hang
To keep the boons thou'rt wonted to receive:
Reproof therein doth hide her venomed fang,
And hard barbaric arts, that mock and grieve.

Here is a stab, and here a mortal thrust ;
Here galley service brought the age to loss ;
Here lies thy virgin forehead rolled in dust
Beside the martyr stake or hero cross.

They who besmirched thy whiteness with their pitch,
Thy gallery of glories did complete ;
They who accepted of thee so grew rich,
Men could not count their treasures in the street.

Thy hollow cheek, and eye of distant light,
Won from the chief of men their noblest love ;
Olympian feasts thy temperance requite,
And thy worn weeds a priceless dowry prove.

I know not if I've caught the matchless mood
In which impassioned Petrarch sang of thee ;
But this I know, — the world its plenitude
May keep, so I may share thy beggary.

KOSMOS.

Of dust the primal Adam came
In wondrous sequency evolved,
With speech that gave creation name,
Of art and artist never solved.

With something of a mother-pang
The Sun conceived the starry spheres
That from her burning bosom sprang, —
Immortal children of her tears.

From height of heat, and stress of span,
The measured Earth took poise and hold :
And beasts, the prophecy of man,
And man, were latent in her mould.

And hid in man a world intense,
The centre point of things that be,
With soul that conquers out of sense
Its incomplete divinity.

Around one infinite intent
All power and inspiration move,
Thrilling with light the firmament,
Lifting the heart of man with love.

FIRST CAUSES.

"WE need no God," the Atheist said ;
" The World is wound, and set to go :
How it was wound we do now know ;
But go it will when we are dead.

You question me as one who pleads
To keep his ancient faith with tears :
In this our harmlessness appears, —
We rob no nature of its needs.

The weak, for whom a God must be,
Will hold the apt invention still,
While from the arbitrary will
We and the hardier souls are free."

Like one who in the dark would walk
Where men by day securely tread,
And stumbles with uneasy dread,
The Atheist blundered in his talk.

Now from my window I survey
This amphitheatre of peace,
Where moon and stars, without surcease,
Nightly present their heavenly play.

I see the beauteous drama wrought;
Its acts and interludes I trace:
I need not seek the Author's face,
Whose spirit visits me unsought.

And what that need, both old and new,
The eternal need of human-kind?
Not that we keep a fable blind:
It is that thou, dear God, be true.

THE CHRIST.

No idle superstition made him;
Nor canst thou, Critic, him unmake;
No sect upreared his holy stature,
Beloved for its divineness' sake.

Wipe rudely out the glowing picture;
Leave but thy blank for man to read;
Write nothingness where'er it please thee;
Take, as I fling them, creed for creed:

What hast thou then? thine own dominion,
The empire that thy nature craves;
Crown thee a tyrant of opinion,
With disbelievers for thy slaves.

He grew not great by priestly cunning,
Nor magic gifts, nor Eastern arts :
Immortal love sprang up to honor
The fair ideal of our hearts.

As from some dreamer's inspiration
Each noble school of Science grew,
And rules that help the striving many
Were moulded from the gifted few;

So, from his life and thoughts transcendent,
Flashed light that ages cannot dim :
Blind Faith and Feeling were before him ;
Religion followed after him.

THE CHURCH.

I HEARD one say in sunny travel,
A braggart Frenchman, rude and vain,
He and his mates would mine St. Peter's,
And blast it with a powder-train.

I saw in thought the mighty ruin,
The wealth of Art and Record gone;
The unfading pictures wrenched and shattered;
The arches, music-knit, o'erthrown.

I thought how piteous Contadini
Would miss that genial mother-hearth;
How, from the falling water-vases,
The marble doves would flutter forth.

Then, from the ghastly vision turning,
Mine eye the silly Celt did reach :
I said, and every heart responded,
" Now, never more with me hold speech."

So thou, whose ill-conditioned learning
Would shake the aisles where Faith abides ;
Where, from the vulgar world out-driven,
Devotion, crowned of ages, hides, —

Wield cautiously the crushing mallet :
Not Peter's door alone you break ;
But, of the temple of our sires,
A weltering heap of dust you make.

These aisles were built with holy living,
These stones were piled with thought and prayer :
The world before us gave the pattern,
The world that follows is the heir ;

And hearts are set, like gems incrusted,
In the fair walls ; and, ruby-red,
The blood of martyrdom doth stain them,
And tears more terrible to shed.

So, build thy dome in airy heaven
A shelter for new hope and joy,
And write thereon the Master-sentence,
" Come to deliver, not destroy."

THE CRUCIFIX.

In desolations of my own
I see a figure lifted lone,
Stript, and extended felon-wise,
That yields not to the solvent skies.

Mother and friends are stolen away;
Fails, too, the cordial light of day;
And Darkness, and the deep Divine,
Their counsels mystical intwine.

The greatest distance cannot hide,
Nor Time, more potent to divide:
Touch but the golden bond of prayer,
He and his agony are there.

The Angel, with the nod of Fate,
Unsmiling and compassionate,
From Life's rude banquet beckoneth
To front us with that crownèd death.

So silent, yet he stirs our veins
To madden for heroic pains;
So passive, turning human-kind,
Leagued with omnipotence of mind.

Uplifting all our weight of woe,
Bringing the vaulted heavens low,
Remembered as the immortal One
Who was, and willed to be, their Son.

KENYON'S LEGACY.

GOOD Johnny Kenyon's gone and done
  The best thing with his money:
He's left it for two Poet-Bees,
  Who make the wasp-world honey.

Unthrifty work, — a world has wants,
  A market-man provides it;
Small wages has the working bee,
  Or the good God who guides it.

But Kenyon knew the market-men,
  And so bestowed his money,
That our two rifled Bees might live
  From henceforth on their honey.

KESTON'S LEGACY

In Casa Guidi, where they dwell,
  They keep the tea-pot waiting;
The precious vapor spends itself
  For their poetic praising.

I know a Western dame who keeps
  The villa styled Negroni,
And whose well-regulated cups
  Are hot to friend and crony.

She says our poets enter like
  A church who brings his steeple;
With visions of the gods they praise,
  They yawn at common people.

When they in turn invite at home,
  The chairs are queer and rotten,
The board is bare, the talk divine,
  The tea-pot long forgotten.

John Kenyon was an Englishman,
    And understood the duty
England expects from English wives,
    Who stand for thrift and beauty.

He did not score it in his will,
    For that had been ungracious;
He told it not by word of mouth, —
    Dependence thrice fallacious.

" 'Tis in the fitness of the thing,
    And they, be sure, will feel it; .
Or else some medial-rapping friend'
    For sixpence may reveal it.

Aurora! dry your pen at night;
    Repose shall help your dreaming;
Enjoy your victuals from this hour,
    And keep your tea-pot steaming."

Like those long-exiled Empire-bees,
    Who now, to fortune coming,
Poise on the topmost bough, and fill
    Your Europe with their humming;

So may you, gold-emblazoned, rest
    On velvet pall and mantle,
Or where luxurious drapings hide
    Time's monitors ungentle.

Or better, build a crystal hive,
    With this remembrance sunny:
"One good man helps the bankrupt world
    To pay our priceless honey."

TO ONE WHO LIES IN FLORENCE.

SHOWER lilies from the skies
Where our lovely Ladye lies!
Birds of more than mortal tune,
Soothe her rest by night and noon;
Angel loves be softly told
O'er her consecrated mould;
Hearts that noblest strive and mean
At her shrine their comforts glean.

Neither may the sun despise
To salute her where she lies,
Nodding over woods and water
To Apollo's crownèd daughter,

Christian Sappho she, whose verse
Holy loving souls rehearse
That a benediction seek
Pontiffs have not grace to speak;

For her bosom temple sweet
Charity did make complete;
Human passions lost their pride
Ranged before the gentle-eyed;
Sword of meekness pierceth deep,
Bitterest chide the eyes that weep;
And her anger humbled most
Through her pity, never lost.

Sister, whose fair lot is cast
Where the shadows of the past
And the sunshine of to-day
Interlace on God's highway.
None of all thy joys I'd ask,
Harnessed gladly to my task.
But the parting kiss she gave,
And the pause beside her grave.

Scatter lilies from the skies,
Shower tears from angels' eyes,
Who forget not that their joy
Our contentment doth destroy.
Nought of earth so good and fair
That beside her may compare ;
Nought of heaven too purely blest
To infold her sinless rest !

THE PRICE OF THE DIVINA COMMEDIA.

GIVE, — you need not see the face,
But the garment hangeth bare;
And the hand is gaunt and spare
That enforces Christian grace.

Many ages will not bring
Such a point as this to sight,
That the world should so requite
Master heart and matchless string.

Wonder at the well-born feet
Fretting in the flinty road.
Hath this virtue no abode?
Hath this sorrow no retreat?

See, beneath the hood of grief,
Muffled bays engird the brow.
Fame shall yield her topmost bough
Ere that laurel moult a leaf.

Give : it is no idle hand
That extends an asking palm,
Tracing yet the loftiest psalm
By the heart of Nature spanned.

In the antechamber long
Did he patient hearing crave :
Smiles and splendors crown the slave,
While the patriot suffers wrong.

Could the mighty audience deign,
Meeting once the inspired gaze,
They should ransom all their days
With the beauty of his strain.

With a spasm in his breast,
With a consummate love alone,
All his human blessings gone,
Doth he wander, void of rest.

Not a coin within his purse,
Not a crust to help his way,
Making yet a Judgment Day
With his power to bless and curse.

Give ; but ask what he has given :
That Posterity shall tell, —
All the majesty of Hell ;
Half the ecstasy of Heaven.

A NEW SCULPTOR.

ONCE to my Fancy's hall a stranger came,
    Of mien unwonted;
And its pale shapes of glory without shame
    Or speech confronted.

Fair was my hall, — a gallery of gods
    Smoothly appointed,
With nymphs and satyrs from the dewy sods
    Freshly anointed.

Great Jove sat throned in state, with Hermes near,
    And fiery Bacchus,
Pallas and Pluto, and those powers of fear
    Whose visions rack us.

Artemis wore her crescent free of stars,
    The hunt just scented;
Glad Aphrodite met the warrior Mars,
    The myriad-tented.

Rude was my visitant, of sturdy form,
    Draped in such clothing
As the world's great, whom luxury makes warm,
    Look on with loathing.

And yet methought his service-badge of soil
    With honor wearing,
And in his dexter hand, embossed with toil,
    A hammer bearing.

But while I waited till his eye should sink,
    O'ercome with beauty,
With heart-impatience brimming to the brink
    Of courteous duty,

He smote my marbles many a murderous blow,
    His weapon poising;
I, in my wrath and wonderment of woe,
    No comment voicing.

"Come, sweep this rubbish from the workman's way,
    Wreck of past ages!
Afford me here a lump of harmless clay,
    Ye grooms and pages!"

Then from that voidness of our mother-earth
    A frame he builded,
Of a new feature, with the power of birth
    Fashioned and welded.

It had a might mine eyes had never seen, —
    A mien, a stature,
As if the centuries that rolled between
    Had greatened Nature.

It breathed, it moved; above Jove's classic sway
    A place was won it:
The rustic sculptor motioned; then "To-day"
    He wrote upon it.

"What man art thou?" I cried, "and what this wrong
    That thou hast wrought me?
My marbles lived on symmetry and song:
    Why hast thou brought me

A form of all necessities, that asks
    Nurture and feeding?
Not this the burthen of my maidhood's tasks,
    Nor my high breeding."

"Behold," he said, "Life's great impersonate,
    Nourished by labor!
Thy gods are gone with old-time faith and fate;
    Here is thy Neighbor."

A VICTIM OF TIBERIUS.

WHAT wouldst thou with me, jailer dark and grim?
My father was Sejanus: this his house,
From which they took him darkly, days ago,
Is mine own home, where I have right to dwell.

Where went my father? He was Cæsar s friend.
But, waiting here, I heard the multitude
Shouting his death, which yet I'll not believe.
And, when they forced my brother from my side,
Still as a ghost he went, and came no more.

See my poor toys spread out before the hearth!
It was a mimic sacrifice I made:
This doll was Iphigenia, this the priest;
And here I pierced my finger, to make blood,

Till my nurse chid me. Are you come for that?
I know our pastime may offend the gods;
Know the dark air is full of whispering things
That bear our follies to the ear of those
Whose wrath is strong, and vengeance terrible.
But I'm not wicked: 'twas no deadly rite
Invoking evil chance on man or God,
Or Cæsar, who is both, they say, in one.
If any power have sent you for my faults,
Which I'll confess as quickly as you'll name,
Bid old Camilla take my mother's rod,
(I had a mother,) she can use it well;
And I'll endure it, though I meant no wrong.

Thou dost not leave me? In thy fearful eyes,
My childhood withers with an instant age.
The marrow of my joints seems long drawn out
Caught on the horror of thy countenance.
Oh! this is like the nightmare that I feared,
Not knowing it could walk abroad by day.
I'd shriek for pity; but my voice is choked,
As if the ashes of the things I love

Stood in my throat to bury utterance.
I must go with thee? Never, while I live.
Ah, pity! by my hair he hurries me
Forth from the palace, through the glaring streets,
That strangely reel, and vanish from my sight.
I see the gods there, black against the sky,
And stiffening with the horror of men's deeds.
The spell that binds my lips is on their hands,
Or they would move to help me. Where is Cæsar?
Now hear this wretch that whispers in mine ear,
"Cæsar will have thy blood." This gives me strength
To snap the chilly net-work of my fear,
And cry, "Thou liest!" See, the Consul comes!
"O noble man! I clasp thy garment's edge:
Save me as thou wouldst save thy fair-haired girl,
My playmate once." Tears darkle in his eyes:
Pale, with a stifled curse he turns away;
He cannot aid me. Where the columns range,
The conscript fathers keep the weal of Rome.
Hark to me, fathers, — I am fatherless!
So quick away? Hear, Tyber, then, my cry;
Hear, ye protecting hills! Ah! silent all.

What's this dark vault? and what yon rusted ring
With the noose dangling? Look to thine own fate!
Thou dar'st not slay a virgin. I will tear
Thine eyes with these small fingers ere thou come
A foot's length nearer! Keep away, away,
Thou untold horror! Only touch me not;
And I will twine thy halter round my throat
Like a bright riband on a festal day.
Give me the rope! let my poor bruised hands go,
Seeking the priceless mercy Death can bring.
Oh, come! since thy still feet are waited for
As the last rapture, — sweet, thou com'st too late.

CAIUS CÆSAR.

I AM the monster Caius, loathed of men, —
Him whose foul record women may not read.
In distant Gaul, an altar to the gods
Attests the mother-pangs that brought me forth,
As I should prove a boon to move them thanks.
My father bred me soldierly in camps;
And the small jack-boots gave my childish name
Caligula. That father, in the East,
Sickened with secret poisons. Ye remember
How wild his widow bore the funeral urn,
Landing at Cyprus? Dark Tiberius then
Drew his death-circle slowly round our way.
My mother, struggling longest, fell at last.
Two brothers followed, — one by hunger's woe;
One by his own resolvèd hand escaped

The hangman's noose, and hooks of infamy.
But I, surviving, kept the tyrant's side
So near, he could not spring to strangle me.
Slowly he recognized my crafty soul,
Knew me his master in all shameful arts,
And, having lopped the fair limbs from the tree,
Left me for the blood-blossoms I should bear,
And fruit of death. At first I only aped
His outward fashions; then I learned his thoughts;
Then his malignant madness seized on me,
And made me like him. Dying as he lay,
I forced the cushion 'twixt his gaping jaws,
And sped his flight from earth. That was, at least,
A service. Could I catalogue my deeds,
Thou couldst not stay to hear them. Hell itself
Swoons at the fatal tale, and cries, "Away!"
My royal ways were tapestried with blood;
First my young brother's, followed by a train
Of ghosts that might become imperial race.
I snatched from new-wed souls their nuptial joys,
And flung them back, disfigured to disgust.
So monstrous and unnatural my lusts,

That the dark horror of the Cæsar's name
Banished the blushing rose of modesty,
And set a ghastly pallor in its place.
My victims were not rashly sped to death,
But tickled with such agony of pain
As gave the stab of dissolution price.
These pleasures wearied, when the thirst for gold
Set in, as cruel and more terrible.
I wrung the hand of toil, whose wretched pence
Gained too much honor in my haughty use.
I saw that vice had profit; wherefore then
I planted it, and gave it ministrance,
As one should tend a vine of fiery growth,
To madden others, and enrich one's self.
To coin, coin, coin, from every bosom's life,
Became my master-thought. Nor was there rest
When darkness hid the busy threads that weave
The color and consistence of men's days.
My dreams were brief. I walked the silent halls,
And plotted murder till the morning came
That made it easy. When I clasped a neck
Close to mine own, I whispered, "Love me well,

Since this fair throat is mine to cut or keep."
All attributions to myself I drew,
All powers, all pleasures, all magnificence.
I clothed in silks and plumes and gems confused.
Now as a woman, now as man, I walked,
Now as a god, with beard of wroughten gold;
And no one chid me, — no one showed a chain,
Or frowned, or threatened as I passed his way.
Beauty was peril, — the fair locks of youth
Were shorn to honor my denuded front.
Where one stood eminent for strength and grace,
I marked him, and the hangman had his word.
Thus did my rivals vanish. All the while,
The slow death ripened in yon treacherous skies,
That looked so blandly, till one burning noon,
All Rome being gathered at the circus sport,
Loosed the swift hand that smote me. As it fell,
A score of poniards, like a shower of stars,
Glittered before me: death was everywhere;
And, hacked and hewed like Julius, I went down.
One shout, the uplifting of a sea of hearts
That praised the gods, was my last sign on earth.

The night before the end of all things came,
I dreamed I sat beside Olympian Jove,
And, reasoning as an equal, blazoned forth
Designs and deeds. "Thus have I done, and thus;
From mine own will, the perfect law of earth.
Hast thou no joy in my magnificence
That goes abroad so glorious, like to thine?
Look at my costly tunic, broidered robe,
Beard of pure gold, and blazing diadem!
Think of my pleasures, boundless as thine own;
My power, like thine, unquestioned, flinging down
Death, and a thousand deaths, for one caprice.
I claim celestial triumph at thine hands:
Here shall they crown me, equal to thyself."
And in my heart I pondered, "Why not greater?"
Thereat the Immortal's front grew dark with wrath,
And, with one sudden spurning of his foot,
He sent me down to earth, precipitate.
Even on this wise, the morrow showed my fall;
But I am now where lower depth is none,
Nor light of Jove, nor human countenance.

Only a company of crownèd ghosts
Fill up the void with wail that never tires,
Who, with a drunken madness like to mine,
Dreamed they were gods, and, waking, were not men.

CLAUDIUS.

WHEN Caius Cæsar sank 'neath righteous steel,
The sweet blue patience of the firmament
Giving full measure, ere Jove's lightning fell, —
Poor Uncle Claudius! the fool, of whom
Augustus wrote, " Let him not sit with us
To see the games; contrive him out of sight
Who shames the Cæsars with his awkward ways," —
He, scorned of men, the butt of all his tribe,
Astonished with the murder, hid his head
In the first truckle-bed he came upon,
Leaving his heels out, by the which they seized,
And dragged him forth. " To death?" he shivering
    cried.
" To empire!" they, and crowned him where he stood.

Not in derision, he gave grace to God,
And spread his solid base of human life.

The ambitious rather tampered with his wives
Than set him on to capering cruelty.
Law did he give, assiduous, all the day;
Though, once, the cook-shop near the judgment-hall
So overcame him, that he slid away,
Feasted him full, and let the sentence wait.
His tastes in blood were moderate, but nice.
He loved to see the Retiarius die,
And therefore bade him lift his quivering face
In the last spasm. Or he would wait a day
The leisure of the executioner
Rather than lose the victim's agonies
The law allowed him.
     With a sudden zeal
He pleaded once the tavern-keeper's cause :
" For who, my masters, would forego his morsel
At the right moment, smoking, brown, and crisp?
And those old wine-shops, with such cool retreats,
And clammy jars, distilling juice divine,

168 *POEMS OF STUDY AND EXPERIENCE.*

Shall we not keep them? Other things must pass:
These good old friends shall stand, Joy's monuments."

He gave the people victuals more than once,
And worthy games, with water combats rare.
Walking abroad, he dubbed them "Dominos,"
His toga loose and slovenly put on,
And offered salutation with his left, —
An act unseemly for a nobleman.
His married life had little luck or skill, —
The second venture wilder than the first,
While the third slew him with his favorite dish,
The stew of mushrooms, dangerous and dear.

Pass on, poor wretch, so dull and debonair, —
This mayst thou teach: How great soe'er the fool,
The multitude's a greater whom he rides.

THE VISION OF PAUL.

WHAT is this that stops my way
Like a wall, unseen by day?
Who doth bid my errand stay
  Ere I come?
What o'erclouds me like a dream,
Blotting each remembered scheme
With an unaccustomed theme?
  " Jèsu sum."

What strange dissolution rends
From the comfort of my friends,
From my life's determined ends?
  Dark and dumb,
What doth bind my fluent tongue

Like an instrument unstrung,
With its lesson never sung?
" Jèsu sum."

See ! this sudden shock of light
Falls like palsy on my sight,
Till I view no path aright
   In my gloom ;
All my faculties are dead,
Every sinew bound with lead :
What this shivering trance of dread?
" Jèsu sum."

" Listen, since for human weal,
That thy misdirected zeal,
Mightier than it murdered, heal,
   Am I come :
Thou with stones my saints hast slain,
Torture bound with scourge and chain ;
Know thyself the martyr pain !
   Jèsu sum.

Thou wert mine without thy knowing;
From this moment's wonder-showing,
Pay the debt thy life is owing
    Burthensome:
On the blindness of thy thought
Dawns the inner life unsought.
Teach, as thou thyself art taught;
    Jèsu sum."

THE GOOD GUALDERALDA.

By Arno, on the Tuscan side,
The matchless Gualderalda grew,
Where many a farm and meadow wide
Her father's domination knew.

He moved in dark and sullen strength;
She grew a lovely flower apart,
With virtues cloistered round her soul,
Like leaflets round the lily's heart.

And now great news the castle stirs:
The King, in hunting, takes this way,
And of your hospitable walls
Will ask his welcome for a day.

"Sir Count, the world accords your house
A daughter marvellously fair :
If I accept your loyal vows,
To see her face shall be my prayer."

Then from her turret near the sky
Came she in blushing maidenhood ;
Then first unveiled before the eye
Of eager admiration stood.

"Sire, you shall touch my daughter's lips
If so your royal pleasure deign ;"
Then paled, in wan and strange eclipse,
Her beauty, with a sudden pain.

"No man shall touch my lips," she saith,
"Save he who claims my wedded hand :
Rather will I resign my breath,
And yield my pulses where I stand."

"How? dost thou mock me, froward girl?"
"Nay, count," the wiser king replies,
"Thou wert a worse than peasant churl
Such unflecked virtue to despise.

Go, Gualderalda, fair indeed!
I'll wed thee proudly in the land:
The noblest knight that crosses steed
Shall claim thy dowry at my hand."

Men note not where her bones repose
In some old crypt, forgotten long;
But Dante keeps her virgin rose
Bright in the chaplet of his song.

1830 AND 1853.

An old man mazed and wild
Bearing a blond-haired child,
A woman blind with tears, —
The mournful train sweeps on ;
And the monarchy is gone
For all the coming years.

They would have lingered slow,
For their hearts beat faint and low,
Their lives were a feeble spoil ;
But the power that's new and strong
Cries, " Hasten them along,
Away from their native soil ! "

But I can stop, and sigh
At this grief of years gone by, —
An old man's fault and fall, —
And say that the exile's woe
Is a piteous thing to know,
Is the heaviest weird of all.

In a palace bare and old
That a royal race left cold,
These children of the sun
Shall moulder in faded state,
Till the sentence, soon or late,
Remove them every one.

Perhaps the shade of her,
For whom brave blood doth stir
To this day in gallant breasts,
Moved through the dusky pile,
And welcomed with sad smile
The old ancestral crests.

The France that gave her birth,
Land of delight and mirth
Her lips were fond to bless,
Rolled this one shattered wave
Across her foreign grave
For very tenderness.

She stands beside his knee,
And, looking wistfully
Upon his reverend head,
Sighs, " Uncle, are you come
From our belovèd home?
'Tis better to be dead!"

O England! glad and free,
With thine own liberty
Endow thy trembling guest ;
Stretch soft thy mantle where
He feels the wintry air,
And fondle him to rest.

But, lo ! a wilder sob,
A swift and mighty throb ;
And towards the rugged North,
With exiled steps of pain,
And fevered eye and brain,
Tis France herself goes forth.

'Tis France ; for 'neath the sun
Freedom and she were one
Five little years ago.
Her glorious flag they fold
As a thing disused and old :
" We have other fashions now."

Her sons must seek their bread,
And lay the weary head
In countries cold and lone ;
Their halls are desolate ;
The friends that made them great,
Their works, and days, are gone.

Nay, never flee, but stand,
Your good sword in your hand,
And cry your watchword true.
Drive the pursuer back:
The foe upon your track
Is mortal, even as you.

His slimy, serpent ways;
His cold, voluptuous days;
His coffers, guilt-increased;
Your fathers' hearths grow cold,
Yourselves in exile old,
That he may reign and feast.

His infant let him fold
In cloth of silk and gold,
Feeding on pearly food:
That child of bastard race,
Let it, too, find a place
In quiet Holy rood.

Flame lights the sunken cheek;
But the exile's hand is weak,
Weightless for good or ill:
Heaven give him sufferance!
But thou, great land of France,
But God, what is thy will?

Oh! never read to-day,
Oh! stretching far away
Where stars revolve and burn, —
The lessons of the free,
The good that is to be,
My children wait to learn.

PERUGIA.

REMEMBER ye Perugia, where Raphael dwelt in years
Whose visions crowded on his brain, ere praise amazed
    his ears;
Where, ripening fast, a Virgin in his master's style he
    drew,
With Babe and Prayer-book in her hands, and heavy
    hood of blue?

Oh! saw you e'er the Switzers stand in helmed and
    jerkined row,
When Christ's meek vicar up the aisle of holy church
    would go?
Bull-necked and brutal-featured they, ferocious, bold
    and strong, —
Their only faith the pound of flesh that's paid for,
    right or wrong.

I've seen them when that church was thronged with
pageants grand and gay ;
When royal rank, and worldly fame, and beauty there
held sway :
The columns wavered in the smoke, the banners hung
aloof,
And the golden song effaced from mind the glories of
the roof.

My soul was drunk with harmony, my senses swam
and reeled :
It may be, when the trump did sound, that down I
sank and kneeled ;
Yet thought I, when I marked those men in cuirass
and in sword,
"How little is the Vicar's state remindful of his
Lord!

No need to keep the people from his mild and harmless way ;
They touched his garments for relief, and were not
warned away ;

And, when his hour of danger came, he put defence to
shame,
Commanding, ' Sheathe again thy sword, or perish by
the same!'"

They came to old Perugia, that helmed and jerkined
pack;
They came with murder in their hearts, and armor
at their back;
They shot the men about the streets, the women at
their fire,
The infant at its mother's knee, child, wife, and aged
sire.

The streets ran blood: in every house some ghastly
corpse was seen.
The passing traveller saved his life by a forgotten
screen;
And, when the fiends have done their work, to Rome
they take their way;
The Pope doth welcome them again, and gladly counts
their pay.

Remember well Perugia, thou Old World and thou
    New!
The Vicar's visitation this, — such care he takes of you,
Ye of no sin accused or tried, warped to no heresy,
Guilty of nothing but the sweet contagion of the free.

Remember, ye who deeply think, and ye who greatly
    dare ;
Remember, ye who talk with God in poesy and
    prayer ;
For he's the lie of all the earth, that false Pope, pride-
    enthroned,
Begirt with flaming cardinals, an idol, serpent-zoned.

'Tis time that Christ should come again, and sweep
    his temple clean,
And rend the glittering robes that hide a fable poor
    and mean.
His Church was not a fortress armed, to deal out death
    and dread ;
Nor yet a mummy sepulchre, where men adore the
    dead :

It was — but ere our creeds grow wise, let once our
 arms be strong
To fling beyond the hating world this monstrous curse
 and wrong.
Sweet Christ, let faithless Peter sink, forgotten, like a
 stone;
And the fair ship move swiftly on, afloat with thee
 alone!

My country, let no hoary lie for refuge come to you!
The things that were have had their day; the things
 that are, are true.
While women kiss the jewelled hand, and praise the
 broidered hem,
Let men bring back the heart of Christ, that lives for
 us and them.

OF WOMAN.

It was a silken woman of the world
That of fond Herod claimed the Baptist's head :
" If this sad virtue gets to countenance,
Our dancing's done with, in the quickest way."
And, for a painted toy, the anointed brow
That knew the Christ's significance must fall.

Such deadly power is hid in smallest things :
The Aspic might have chilled from Love's delight
The bosom it assisted to Love's end.
The shaft of death is subtle as a thread, —
The air may bring, the garland's bloom conceal, —
One desperate finger holds it over us,
Or in a woman's snowy breast it lies.

Teach, then, the woman all the Prophet's worth,
So will she bow the tresses of her head
To yield him passing homage, and pour out
The treasure of her life to ransom his.

I love the woman with the woman's heart,
Giving, not gathering, — shedding light abroad
As the man glooms it in, for midnight toil.
Better our Hebrew Eve, who shares with love
The guilty glory of her stolen prize,
Than the three haughty Heathen who rose up,
Claiming of man a vain pre-eminence, —
Not his to give, — God's only, and the heart's.

They showed me drawings by a six-years' child
Of beasts incongruous, harnessed to a car:
" Now, on my life, he is artist-born," I said.
" Wherefore? You see the slim camelopard
Rearing her strength up, pulling from the head;
While the swift horses stretch to twice their length,
Spinning themselves to slender threads of speed,
Nay, with their iron sinews knitting up

A belt of haste like that our Shakspeare drew
With Puck's impatient malice, round the world.
The little one has guessed the trick of strength
And action, so is artist-born," I say.

" For your true artist knows how all things work ;
Bestows no Zephyrus to prop a pile
Whose angles huge insult his littleness,
Cramping the sympathetic soul with pain,
But the great patient forms whose shoulders broad
Invite such burthens ; whose fixed features say,
' This weight contents us ; we are glad in strength ;'
While the light figure poises at the top,
Holding the heavy network gathered up
To meet the apex of his graciousness.

So, Sisters, leave the weightier tasks of strength,
The underpinnings of society,
And flutter with your graces nearer heaven.
He thinks of you, the steadfast Caryatid, —
The faithful arches clasp their hands beneath

To keep you in your breathless eminence ;
The gloomy cellar way, the weary stair,
Exalt the platform where you reign serene.

Stay there, Beloved, the Angel at the top,
That crowns and lightens all the heavy work.
The very prisoners, entering at the grate,
Perceive an intercession in thine eyes,
And keep their dungeons, waiting for thy sword.
Stay thus, my Angel, seeing over thee
The Heaven that dreamed the Mary and her Christ,—
The dream whereat the Baby Earth awoke,
And, smiling, keeps that smile forever more."

AMANDA'S INVENTORY.

This is my hat: behold its upstart plume,
Soaring like pride, that even in heaven asks room!
This is my cloak of scarlet splendor rare,
A saucy challenge to the sunset glare.

Behold my coach of state and pony chaise,
A fairy pleasure for the summer days;
The steeds that fly, like lightnings in a leash,
With their rude Jove, subservient to my wish.

Here are my jewels; each a fortune holds;
A starving artist planned the graceful moulds:
Here hang my dresses in composed array,
A rainbow with a hue for every day.

These are my lovers, registered in date,
Who, with my dowry, seek myself to mate.
The haughtiest wooer wins me for his bride :
Who asks affection? Pride should wed with pride.

These are my friends, who hourly come or send,
Pleased with my notice and a finger-end ;
Yonder's my parson, proud to share my feast ;
My doctor's there, a sycophantic beast.

This is my villa, where I take my ease
With flowers well-ordered, and ambitious trees ;
And this — what sudden spectre stays my breath?
Amanda, poor Amanda ! this is death.

LYKE-WAKE.

I saw him at a banquet gay,
Elate with speech and flushed with wine:
Above the revel making way,
His eye, unwitting, answered mine.

What his expressed I did not read;
But mine, if I mistake not, said,
" This minds me of their feasts indeed
Who drain the wine-cup o'er their dead;

Who set the liquid fire to flare
Where late the spirit-flame has flown;
The sorrow still unearthed and bare
The miserable drink should drown."

BARGAINS.

He prest a ruby on her lips, whose burning blood
    shone through ;
Twin sapphires bound above her eyes, to match their
    fiery blue ;
And, where her hair was parted back, an opal gem he
    set, —
Type of her changing countenance, where all delights
    were met.

" Will you surrender now," he said, " the ancient
    grudge you keep
Untiring and unutterèd, like murder in the deep?"
" I thank you for the word," she said ; " your gems
    are fair of form
But when did jewels bind the depths, or splendors
    still the storm?

There is no diamond in the mine, nor pearl beneath
    the wave,
There is no fretted coronet that soothes a princely
    grave,
There is nor fate nor empire in the wide infinity,
Can stand in grace and virtue with the gift you had
    from me."

ROUGE GAGNE.

The wheel is turned, the cards are laid;
The circle's drawn, the bets are made:
I stake my gold upon the red.

The rubies of the bosom mine,
The river of life, so swift divine,
In red all radiantly shine.

Upon the cards, like gouts of blood,
Lie dinted hearts, and diamonds good,
The red for faith and hardihood.

In red the sacred blushes start
On errand from a virgin heart,
To win its glorious counterpart.

The rose that makes the summer fair,
The velvet robe that sovereigns wear,
The red revealment could not spare.

And men who conquer deadly odds
By fields of ice, and raging floods,
Take the red passion from the gods.

Now, Love is red, and Wisdom pale,
But human hearts are faint and frail
Till Love meets Love, and bids it hail.

I see the chasm, yawning dread;
I see the flaming arch o'erhead:
I stake my life upon the red.

THE TEA-PARTY.

I AM not with you, sisters, in your talk ;
I sit not in your fancied judgment-seat :
Not thus the sages in their council walk,
Not in this wise the calm great spirits meet.

My life has striven for broader scope than yours ;
The daring of its failure and its fact
Have taught how deadly difficult it is
To suit the high endeavor with an act.

I do not reel my satire by the yard,
To flout the fronts of honorable men ;
Nor, with poor cunning, underprize the heart
Whose impulse is not open to my ken.

Ah! sisters, but your froward speech comes well
To help the woman's standard, new-unfurled:
In carpet council ye may win the day;
But keep your limits, — do not rule the world.

What strife should come, what discord rule the times,
Could but your pettish will assert its way!
No lengthened wars of reason, but a rage,
Shown and repented twenty times a day.

Ye're all my betters, — one in beauty more,
And one in sharpness of the wit and tongue,
And one in trim, decorous piety,
And one with arts and graces ever young.

But well I thank my father's sober house
Where shallow judgment had no leave to be,
And hurrying years, that, stripping much beside,
Turned as they fled, and left me charity.

MAID AND MISTRESS.

AN ECLOGUE.

LADY OLYMPIA, I'm so glad you've left
The dreary villa for this pleasant home
That lies in sight of every omnibus,
And sends the winds that whistle as they pass
To vent their spite elsewhere, — so stout it is.

Here, too, are men to tramp the stairs for us,
The sort of men that care for women's thanks.
Your country louts, you know, are country-bred :
No mother-feeling, stirring at the heart,
Sends them to help us at the wood or well.

Then, so communicable with the shops !
The butcher comes, the baker also comes,
And at a nod the grocer's boy is here ;

While from my cousin's uncle's brother's wife
I hear of neighbors, and the folks at home.

You sigh, dear lady; for you loved your fields,
And talked of Nature, which I never learned,
Seeking the sunny corners all day long;
Or, sitting grand and graceful in the hall,
Kept still a blazing log to comfort you,
While we went shivering up the garret stairs,
Asking each night, " When will my lady move?"

Ah! mistress dear, I love your service well,
And praise it with the honest bread I eat:
But you're too easy with our sort of folk;
And that great cook, the red-faced, humbugs you.

The man too — why, his eyes will dance with mirth
When you receive his solemn tale of work,
Looking such pity for his aching joints;

He having sat beside the kitchen fire,
And munched his victuals thankless, all the day,
While we, poor womankind, have hauled the coals,
And brought the water up, with straining backs,
Till he has grown ashamed to meet our looks,
And feigned a villanous sleep to shut them out.

Well, well, you're snug within your chamber now,
And I have company, and needful help,
And beautiful oak-chips to light your fire;
And so the winter promises to pass:
But, Dame Olympia, let me rule the cook,
And keep her cousins from the larder shelf,
All fond of her, and blest with appetite.

And should that louting Thomas rouse himself,
Never say, "Thomas, do not work so hard;"
For when you speak so, and I bid him wag,
He'll answer, "Did you mind my mistress' words?
I'm sitting here to help her care of me."

Thus spake my favorite, petted by long love;
And I forgave that neighborhood of stars,
And softest quarrel 'twixt the shore and sea,
Which made my villa, where you've sat at meat
With little splendor, worthy of a queen.

THE MODERATE MAN.

How shall the money flow into my pocket?
Swift grow the fortunes of men, and their pride.
Small my estate, though I labor to stock it,
Left of my father, fourfold to divide.

Money to dress these fair girls of mine finely,
Catch a rich suitor, and rivet him fast;
Couches of silk to repose on supinely,
Wooing the life-joys gone by with the past.

Soon my young master asks horses to ease him,
Saucy at college, at billiards most brave;
Endless devices shall plunder and please him.
Youth must have follies, and parents can save.

. . . . . .

Nay, thou art pampered e'en now out of measure,
Lackest no comfort through hunger or grief;
Dances and festivals bring needless pleasure,
Seen to depart with a sigh of relief.

See where my lost ones sit low in their mourning,
Sunken the bosom, and hollow the cheek;
There may thy spirit find better adorning
With the inheritance vowed to the meek.

Seeking the boasting, the tinsel, the racket,
Little thou learn'st Life's miraculous art:
Let the gold rather flow out of thy pocket;
Then may the mercy flow into thy heart.

WARNING.

Power, reft of aspiration ;
Passion, lacking inspiration ;
Leisure, not of contemplation.

Thus shall danger overcome thee,
Fretted luxury consume thee,
All divineness vanish from thee.

Be a man, and be one wholly ;
Keep one great love, purely, solely,
Till it make thy nature holy ;

That thy way be paved in whiteness,
That thy heart may beat in lightness,
That thy being end in brightness.

CONTRASTS.

I SHALL not come to the heavenly court
As I enter your ball to-night,
In tissues wreathed with flowery sport,
And jewels of haughty light,

Bearing on shoulders stiff and straight
The marble of my face,
Moving with high and measured gait
To claim my yielded place.

Poor narrow souls! your easy spite
Moves this enforced disdain:
I cannot vanish from the fight
Other than crowned or slain.

The russet garb of penitence
  For me were lighter wear
Than all a queen's magnificence,
  A prince's minivère.

Unloose, unloose your chains of pride,
  Set my vexed spirit free,
That I may follow my angel guide
  In glad humility.

For I would hearken the sentence deep,
  Abide the lifted rod,
And sink, like a chastened child, to weep
  In the fatherhood of God.

A VISION OF PALM SUNDAY.

IF I were a titled princess, this blessèd Palm-Sunday morn,
I'd not sit in this little carriage, with varnish and paint forlorn;
Nor wear this old cloak and bonnet, kept carefully for the day:
There should be no best in my wardrobe; I'd go in best things alway.

And this Yankee should never drive me, this saucy son of the whip,
Who sits in a cart on week-days, a leather belt on his hip;
Nor this small horse of smaller breeding, that starts at each foolish fright:
I'd borrow the Sun's proud coursers, and sweep through the streets like light.

This dust should not trouble my vision, nor smart in
    my tingling breast;
With dewy drops rosy scattered, the air itself should
    be blest;
And these people that stare so wanly from their win-
    dows empty of sky
Should glow like a sun-touched landscape with the joy
    of my riding by.

For you see, I myself should bless them; no committee
    should scan their need:
I'd visit their doleful dwellings, my help should be help
    indeed;
I'd bring them to true heart-wishes, not only to clothes
    and bread;
I'd pull down these toppling houses, and build pretty
    cots instead.

And this were my April fooling, when they came from
    this morning's church, —
In vain for their rags and cobwebs, and joyless beds,
    should they search:

All waving with snowy curtains their newly stained
　　walls should be ;
And their scores paid up at all dealers, such help
　　should they claim from me.

And these little ones bare and ragged, that play with
　　the Sunday's palms,
They should answer with wide-mouthed wonder, I'd
　　give them such golden alms ;
And these crying babies some angel should touch with
　　a waving bough,
Till they smiled on their mothers' bosoms, where they
　　hang so heavily now.

But not such poor cheap-bought comforts, not blessings
　　that come for pelf, —
The dearest and costliest blessing, I'd carry it in my-
　　self.
My smile should be meed for heroes, my lips draw
　　such tender breath,
That a little strain of my music should comfort the
　　pangs of death.

Such a heart I'd bear in my bosom, that, threading the
 crowded streets,
My face should shed joy unlooked for on every poor
 soul one meets ;
And such wisdom should crown my forehead, that,
 coming where counsels stand,
I should carry the thoughts of justice, and stablish the
 weal of the land.

The servants that waited on me should so prize the
 gracious task,
No wage-gold should bring or bind them, my presence
 were all to ask ;
And they who should leave my service, with sorrowful
 feet and slow
Out-lengthening a dear remembrance, from my sight
 and sound should go.

For a church I'd have such a temple as wonders the
 world in Rome,
With a thousand sunny corners where angels might
 make their home:

I'd not have the prayers in Latin, and the doctrine far
out of reach,
But the homely to help the humble, like the Fisher of
old should preach.

For myself I would keep no gewgaws, no trumpery
cloth of gold,
No stick of a Stick in Waiting for gaping fools to
behold :
Friends should gather where'er I wandered, hearts
should build me a blood-red throne ;
'Tis with loving the world and with blessing I'd win
it to be my own.

Yet I'd keep the rich guerdon of beauty, and youth
should but mellow down
To a fuller, maturer feeling, that knowledge and duties
crown ;
And the tireless flow of spirits, with the sober delight
of art,
And some subtle, saintly secret, to hold from the world
apart.

If thy wealth be loving and giving, the good God is
 over all
To bless the world with thy blessing, — no prayer doth
 unheeded fall.
Gather back thy joys in thy bosom this blessèd Palm-
 Sunday morn,
For we have the grace that we ask for; thou'rt better
 than princess born.

JEALOUSY.

Low in my bosom, aspic, thou must hide,
Its best blood not too dainty for thy fang;
Such closeness saves me from the hell of pride,
Should haughty conquerors know the deadly pang.

No beggar takes thee home. In all men's eyes
I have been crowned with glory in my time :
Joy that made Envy cruel to a crime
Has draped me in the sight of summer skies.
And she who flouts me, fallen from my prime,
Had been a spot upon my affluent noon
That grasped the hill-tops, and the valleys drew
To one accord of rapturous delight.

Ah me! in love, December waits on June :
We have not lost a gesture nor a tune,
Before a rival revels in our right.

Sting deep to death, that sex and soul be lost,
That they, the happy, may turn cold with shame ;
Love, to recall his gem of worthier cost ;
And Hate, to find me perished ere she came.

WITHOUT AND WITHIN.

Go away to the world's wild hubbub :
I cannot go with thee ;
For the deep home-anchors hold me
From the waves of that yeasty sea,
Where, the sun my fresh sail gilding,
We once held company.

If the vain and the silly bind thee,
I cannot unlock thy chain ;
If sin and the senses blind thee,
Thyself must endure the pain ;
If the arrows of conscience find thee,
Thou must conquer thy peace again.

Here the line that runs between us
Is narrow, but black as night:
Faith sits passive this side the border,
More happy, perhaps, than sight;
And I wring me slow drops of comfort
Where once I drank swift delight.

For I sit here with lovelorn Tasso;
With Dante, hooded and crowned;
While, further, the classic satyrs
Beat the old Virgilian ground;
And I hark for the Flaccian lyre,
Till spirit comes back for sound.

Here I sit with the scornful Roman
Who tells his grim tale so cold
Of the vanishing Southern nation,
And the Northerns bright-haired and bold:
Last year 'twas a breathless story,
But now 'tis a tale oft told.

And the sons of Science around me
Reach help from reservèd hands:
They have spread their net for the Godhood,
And bound Him with close-wove bands,
While He counts their small thoughts in His balance
With minutes, and drops, and sands.

I am here with the prophets whose warnings
In the golden eternity fall;
I am here with the good Physician
Who healeth both great and small;
I am here with the great soul-masters;
And sorrow, greater than all.

THE VOICE OF THE CATARACT.

CANOPIED by trees, the Torrent
Rages on her bed of stone;
She, so slim and staid last summer,
To a monstrous madness grown.

At her feet the fair Spray children,
Tossing wide their snowy locks,
Cushion soft her frantic movements
From the roughness of the rocks.

What doth ail thee, hoary Princess,
Tossing on thy bed of pain,
While the ruddy trees above thee
Drop unceasing tears of rain?

Fain to loose thy pallid tresses,
Fain thy garments wild to tear, —
Like a passion, ever moving;
Like a sorrow, ever there.

Was the summer wind thine Essex?
Did some treacherous blossom-pile
Keep his last sigh from thy bosom,
From his sight thy pardoning smile?

" Oh the bitter frost of winter!
Oh the false delight of spring!
He whose heart knows no betrayal
Skills not of the song I sing."

THE EVENING RIDE.

THROUGH purple clouds with golden crests
I go to find my lover;
Hid from my sight this many a year,
My heart must him discover:
I know the lair of the timid hare,
The nest of the startled plover.

O Earth! of all thy garlands keep
The fairest for our meeting:
Could we ask music, 'twere to drown
The heart's tumultuous beating,
That only eyes, in glad surprise,
Might look through tears their greeting.

If Time have writ my beauty out,
I have no charm to blind him;
No snare to catch his doubting soul,
Nor vow exchanged to bind him;
But this I keep, that I must weep
Bitterly when I find him.

NIGHT-MUSINGS.

I WALK the lonely roofs at night,
The roof-tree creaking as I go ;
A farthing taper gives me light,
And monstrous darkness sits below.

What spell is in these feet of mine
That binds them so to beat the air?
What tears are in my blood, or wine,
That will not yield to sleep or prayer?

Ah me ! the day brought sleep enough ;
Its humming pulses drowsed my soul ;
My ways were spun of funeral stuff,
And every meal was death and dole.

But now my measured footstep seems
A chariot, drawn by burning doves;
Or now my fancy climbs in dreams
A ladder of transfigured loves.

Or now I stand as Jacob stood,
Matched hand to hand, and knee to knee:
Thou unknown Fate, declare thy good!
Answer, and I will set thee free.

And now I walk a garden bed,
Whose flowers contend with fervent airs;
And each fair bell that lifts its head
A look of loved remembrance wears.

Or, last, I sit in some strange isle,
Unsexed by Age and Wisdom's might,
And make a pictured parchment smile
With words illegible for light.

A slip, a shock, a distant tone !
The world's pale watchman crying woe ;
I spin my thread of light alone,
And Darkness whets its shears below.

SUMMER NIGHT.

IN the lovely summer night,
Softest music breathes around me,
Softest memories have bound me,
In the lovely summer night.

A Star doth send his light, —
A blazing diamond, pearl beset,
The brightest where the bright are met,
In the lovely summer night.

In the lovely summer night, —
Walking with beloved shadows
O'er the star-lit heaths and meadows
In the lovely summer night.

SUMMER NIGHT.

In the lovely summer night,
Sharp-edged Sorrow waits to seize me;
Death, from sorrow to release me
In the lovely summer night.

EROS HAS WARNING.

SHUT here thy burning gospel;
Thou and I must part, O Love!
Keep ambush for youth's gay spirits
To bear in thy car above;
Leave me slow to tread the earth-ball,
Who languidly live and move.

Wait not with thy wings where I issue
In the winter's cold and frost,
To carry me swift through the snow-drift,
And the heavens, cloud-embossed:
I will take me a humbler airing,
Will travel at lowlier cost.

Thou foe of the task and the fireside,
Thou foe of the placid brow,
Thou tyrant of gentlest bosoms,
Seek other dominion now!
For my years lie counted before me;
I must work to redeem a vow.

When thou passest, all in thy glory,
With thy rosy-bosomed crew;
When thy Pæan loud resoundeth,
And the World is crowned anew, —
I'll not join the frantic strophe,
I'll not sing " Io" too.

A web of peace and of science
Hangs gathering in my loom,
And I work after thoughts of wisdom
That blot out our human doom;
And the garb I have wrapped around me —
I shall carry it to the tomb.

So here I acknowledge, master,
Thy magical law and spell;
Oh! deeper than thought can fathom,
Oh! greater than words can tell;
Let us part from our hands' long clasping,
And solemnly bid farewell.

EROS DEPARTS.

Love that wert my being,
Love that passest death,
Am I here without thee,
Breathing human breath?
Moving, not to meet thee
On this summer morn?
While the Earth, new-cinctured,
Blyth and bloom adorn?

While the deep-hung branches,
Trailing, sweep the ground,
And the droning beetle
Spinneth round for round,

And the light, wave-broken,
Shimmers on the sea,
Do I sit here, waiting
Nevermore for thee?

But for thee my fancy
Chose these garments white,
Wove the tufted roses
But for thy delight;
But for thee this diamond,
Darling of the mine,
Glistens in the ear-drop
Like a tear of thine, —
Like a tear, that, welling
From thy happy breast,
Where thy vows were whispered,
Waiteth to be blest.

Beasts in yonder meadow
Lightly choose a mate,
Missing, scarce a day's length
Wonder they, and wait;

But the ewe lamb's mother
Bleateth long and sore ;
Thrush, in yonder covert,
Sorroweth evermore ;
Choking with a spasm
In her silver strain,
" Dear delight of summer,
Come again, again ! "

Not that thou shouldst leave me, —
Thou, ethereal born ;
But that I survive thee, —
That is grief and scorn.

Poor in form and stature,
Pale and dull of hue,
By thy creed of beauty
Towards thy wish I grew,
Fought with Time and Nature,
Conquered bitter pain,
Keeping thievish footsteps
From thy dear domain.

From that task delightsome,
Grief-absolved I lie;
Free to pine and perish,
Love, since thou canst die.
While the trees, like mourners,
Bear my azure pall,
Let the whirlwind scatter,
Let the ashes fall,
Striving towards no heaven
Dim and distant far:
Only where thou dwellest
The Immortals are.

SIMPLE TALES.

I.

WHAT are they bringing to this grave,
O Sexton pale and old?
What blossom white, or blasted root,
Must underlie this mould?
Hark to the bell! — I cannot tell:
We dig the grave, and ring the knell.

If you must ask — that married pair,
That move so stiff and sad,
With snow-flakes thickening in their hair,
In new-dyed sables clad;
The kerchief busy at their eyes,
That way, methinks, the burthen lies.

In yonder moss-clad church, their pew
Showed once a gracious child,
A laughing imp of rosy hue
In glee and mischief wild.
To manhood grown, he went away,
Returning in an evil day.

" Ho, rascals ! " cries he, " take my beast ;
Haste there, and let me in ;
My father keeps a sorry feast,
My mother's sour and thin.
I've come to change their ways a bit ;
Fetch brandy, fill a bumper fit !

Squire, I have debts in yonder town ;
I fling the careless card ;
My tradesmen press their bills, and frown ;
My creditors are hard.
This world is not a mother's breast,
No cradle, for a babe to rest."

The mother scans him in the light
Of the oriel deep and wide.
Where are those curls and dimples bright,
The cheek, her blushing pride?
Whose touch could smooth that tangled hair,
Now knotted, like a snaky snare?

Nor this the worst: the bloodshot eye;
The voice of scoffing tone;
The lips unsteady, that defy
The pleading of her own.
In grief she struggles and sinks down:
He answers with a sullen frown.

The unwilling gold is quickly brought,
And, silent, counted out;
The seeker has the boon he sought,
And flushing turns about.
The mother speaks not to deplore;
The father whispers, " Come no more.

Your sister's portion here you take,
Your mother's jointure too :
Though all were beggared for your sake,
It would not furnish you."
" Oh ! take it all," the mother cries,
And follows him with streaming eyes.

I know this only, since that time
A year or so has past.
But seeds of misery and crime
Ripen unearthly fast.
The Hall's entailed, that cannot go ;
But there they keep with little show.

And when I heard, three days agone,
A young man at the inn
Had, desperate, shut himself alone,
And died the death of sin,
I said, " The Squire has lost his son ;
Wife, there's a grave must be begun."

How came this? through some hidden vein
Of wildness in the blood,
That penitence and deadly pain
Could turn him not to good :
So, when his drunken fury went,
He might not bear his ill-content.

Old man with burning eyes and hair
Like ashes over flame,
Look not too sternly on the heir
Of deeper than thy name :
Thy fiery youth, its guilt, its gains,
Ran their traditions in his veins.

Nor wanted he an angel friend ;
Still in his clouded eyes,
With hope and promise run to end,
His mother's look would rise,
So prayer might bless his parting breath,
And faith, long banished, come in death.

II.

He loved her long through grief and pain,
As long she loved another.
Life was to him her sole domain ;
He was to her a brother.

When well of love he urged and spake,
Tears on her eyelids glistened ;
The heart his wooing strove to wake
Forsook him while she listened.

Thus in a mutual twofold search
Each deeper led the other.
She was his wealth, his law, his church ;
He was to her a brother.

God took him in his early years,
Ere half his youth had flowered.
Then she beheld him through her tears
With the heart's saints embowered.

Time on her heart's high daring smiled,
A blooming bridal made her,
And, clinging to a three-hours' child,
In the low furrow laid her.

But to my sight doth crowned appear
Each faithful, fond endeavor :
Ralph called her his, one happy year ;
And Herbert, his forever.

THE ROSE IN THE JOURNAL.

Rose, whose matchless beauty
Poets love to praise,
Bind the day that brought him
To the other days;
To the homely duties;
To the things that are,
Like dark weights of nature
Linked to sun and star.

Then the curtain lifted
Of the tent so gray
Showed him fresh and blooming
As careering Day,
Ere his steeds are wearied
With the noontide heat,
Ere the lengthening shadows
Press his loitering feet.

Like an Angel's garment
Caught in fluttering grasp;
Like a kingly jewel
Set in costliest clasp;
Like a sudden vision
Of the joys that were,
When the shadows darken
And the end draws near,—

Thus among my treasures,
Rosebud, thou shalt lie,
With thy beauty withering
Only to the eye.

Roses grow immortal
On the brow of Fame:
These, with all best glories,
Deathless keep thy name.

A DREAM OF DISTANCE.

COLDLY sunk, as the pearl in the wave,
Is the love I have borne to thee :
Over its stillness the waters lave
Darkly, silently, heavily.

All the chances under the sun
Scarce can give that the sunken pearl
See the light of the star she loves,
Lifted out of the water's whirl.

Of all the chances under the sun,
For that one I'll ne'er seek nor pray :
Let me lie where the tides move on ;
Thou, bright Lucifer, keep thy way !

For the mystical pulse of life
Holds in sympathy divine
Things apart, like the star and pearl;
Things akin, like thy soul and mine.

FAME AND FRIENDSHIP.

THE world doth name thee now, and idle men
Exalt their critic skill in praising thee:
At all their words my heart doth bound again;
And praise begetteth praise, as this should be.

Yet I remember with a jealous love
What time thine unmined wealth lay less in view;
And I was fain the envious clods to move,
And point the hidden diamonds clear as dew.

Methought men's souls, unquestioning of art,
Were then as void of pulse as stock or stone;
Yet, gathering all thy glories in my heart,
My slender trump uplifted them alone.

So, when the arena rings with plaudits loud,
Hear my heart's whisper through the noisy throng;
And let thy fancies, running o'er the crowd,
Pause where the rites of gratitude belong.

For I have been a mother to thy fame,
Coaxing with gentle touch the grasp of Fate;
Till, holding high the blazon of thy name,
I cried to all the world, "*He shall be great!*"

A WOMAN'S PRAYER.

FATHER of great mercy! hear me mildly:
One I love is tried and hindered sore;
For the harrows of temptation wildly
Tear his green and blooming purpose o'er.

Send thine angels, as the Spring her beauties
Rains on thorny branches wild and scar,
Lighting up Life's worn and wintry duties
With the glories they were made to bear.

Send them in the panoply of heaven
Like a cohort sheathed in burnished gold;
Send them thick as falling dews of even
With soft arms to shelter and infold.

Send them, while I coin my life as ransom
For the holy triumph they must win;
Take the uncounted pulses of my bosom;
Keep the thing I love from deadly sin.

Slow the answer gathers, " Stay thy pleading;
From his birth my help around him lies:
He, the angel in his breast unheeding,
Should escape the legions of the skies."

THE LAST BIRD.

LITTLE Bird that singest
Far atop this warm December day,
    Heaven bestead thee, that thou wingest,
Ere the welcome song is done, thy way

    To more certain weather,
Where, built high and solemnly, the skies,
    Shaken by no storm together,
Fixed in vaults of steadfast sapphire rise!

    There the smile that mocks us
Answers with its warm serenity;
    There the prison-ice that locks us
Melts forgotten in a purple sea.

There thy tuneful brothers,
In the palm's green plumage waiting long,
   Mate them with the myriad others,
Like a broken rainbow bound with song.

Winter scarce is hidden,
Veiled within this fair, deceitful sky:
   Fly, ere, from his ambush bidden,
He descend in ruin swift and nigh!

By the Summer stately,
Truant, thou wast fondly reared and bred:
   Dost thou linger here so lately,
Knowing not thy beauteous friend is dead,—

Like to hearts, that, clinging
Fervent where their first delight was fed,
   Move us with untimely singing
Of the hopes whose blossom-time is sped?

Beauties have their hour,
Safely perched on the spring-budding tree :
For the ripened soul is trust and power.
And beyond, the calm eternity.

FAREWELL TO HAVANA.

My sight is blank, my heart is lorn ;
My tropic trance of joy I mourn, —
That stolen summer of delight,
Dreamed on the breast of wintry night,
When sad, true souls abide the North,
And we, love-truants, issued forth
To find, with steady sail unfurled,
The glowing centre of the world.

The glorious sights went fleeting by ;
I had no hold on earth or sky :
Two little hands, one helpless heart,
Could claim and keep so small a part.
A shadow of the stately palm ;
A burnish of the noontide calm ;

A dream of faces new and strange,
Darkened and lit with sudden change;
A joy of flowers unearthly fair
In giant Nature's tangled hair;
A joy of fruits of other hue
And savor than my childhood knew;
A sorrow, as the vista grew,
Longer and lesser, cherished too;
A pang of parting, heart-bereft
Of all I had, — is all I've left.

To cheer my journey what remains
Towards the rude heights where Winter reigns?
What love-nursed thought shall shield my breast
Warmer than cloak or sable vest?
One hope serene all comfort brings, —
Who made thy bonds did lend thy wings;
Who sends thee from this faery reign
Once brought thee here, and may again.

A WILD NIGHT.

THE storm is sweeping o'er the land,
   And raging o'er the sea :
It urgeth sharp and dismal sounds,
   The Psalm of Misery.

The straining of the cordage now,
   The creaking of a spar,
The deep dumb shock the vessel feels
   When billows strike and jar, —

It breathes of distant seamen's hearts
   That think upon their wives ;
Of wretches clinging to the mast,
   And wrestling for their lives.

The clouds are flying through the sky
  Like spectres of affright:
Yon pale witch moon doth blast them all
  With bleared and ghastly light.

Great Demons flutter through the dark
  Flame touched, with dusky wing;
And Passion crouches out of sight
  Like a forbidden thing.

The blast doth scourge the forest through,
  Great oaks, and bushes small;
And God, the fable of the fools,
  Looks silently on all.

Oh! if He watches, as I know,
  Safe let Him keep our rest,
And give my little ones and me
  The shelter of His breast.

No harm shall come on earth, we trust;
But, if mischance must be,
Most let him help those weary souls
That struggle with the sea!

BABY'S SHOES.

"And it came to pass, that as we ascended the stair, at bedtime, we encountered the baby's shoes, which the mother kissed, and put in her bosom."

LITTLE feet, pretty feet,
   Feet of fairy Maud,
Fair and fleet, trim and neat,
   Carry her abroad!

Be as wings, tiny things,
   To my butterfly:
In the flowers, hours on hours,
   Let my darling lie.

Shine ye must, in the dust,
   Twinkle as she runs,
Threading a necklace gay
   Through the summer suns.

Stringing days, borrowing phrase,
    Weaving wondrous plots,
With her eyes blue and wise
    As forget-me-nots.

Like a charm which doth arm
    Some poor mother's pain
For the child dream-beguiled
    She shall know again,

By the pet amulet
    Kept through lonely years ;
Little shoe, I and you
    Would not part for tears.

Cinderel grown a belle,
    Coming from her ball,
Frightened much, let just such
    A tiny slipper fall.

If men knew as I do
Half thy sweets, my own,
They'd not delay another day,
I should be alone.

Come and go, friend and foe,
Fairy Prince most fine!
Take your gear otherwhere;
Maud is only mine.

MOTHER'S NONSENSE.

WHERE are the eyes of the Lovely One, —
The sweet blue eyes of the Lovely One?
    Oh! here they shine
    To comfort mine,
The cloudless eyes of the Lovely One.

Where are the hands of the Lovely One, —
The tiny hands of the Lovely One?
    They grasp the air,
    So small and fair,
Seeking angel's fingers, my Lovely One!

Where is the mouth of the Lovely One, —
The cunning mouth of the Lovely One?
    I kiss it so,
    It cannot say no,
The sweet wee mouth of the Lovely One.

And where is the place of the Lovely One, —
The happy place of the Lovely One?
   On mother's knee
   High throneth he ;
And her heart is the home of the Lovely One.

THE BABE'S LESSON.

I was saying "Avè, avè,"
    Over a lost delight,
When Baby, scarce five moonlights old,
    Looked up with wondering sight.
    Then his untutored organ
    Caught up the tragic tone,
And with my spent sigh blended soft
    A music of its own.

    I was weary of my burthen,
    Desiring not to be;
When thus unto my thoughts discoursed
    The babe upon my knee:
"Why, mother, sighing ever?
    What boots thy cherished woe?
What matter through the mighty sea
    If sweet or bitter flow?

Behold thy gallant champion,
New lighted from the skies!
Strong arm and word, and heart of cheer,
Are in him, blossom-wise.
A man, and he who wrongs me
Escapes his lesson not;
But who should grieve my mother's heart
Must dearly pay the scot.

Then wait, thou silly mother,
The days till I am grown:
Thou knowest a many heart like thine
Doth keep its watch alone.
Set up Prayer's golden ladder
That brings the heaven-sent joy;
And with sweet hope and patient faith
Nourish thy tender boy."

"I will, I will, my dearest,
Else 'twere unblest to live;
The heaven is wide above our head,
And God is free to give.

But I was not weeping, baby,
Nor raising a hand of might;
I was only saying Avè
Over a lost delight."

"SERVANT TO A WOODEN CRADLE."

Come, visit the flowers, thy cousins,
God's dear little lamb, and mine!
See where, lit by one flaming crystal,
The gems of the greenhouse shine!
The leaves of this rose thou shalt scatter
With the strength of thine infant will:
Thou hast ravished the form of the flower,
See! the heart keeps its sweetness still.

The flowers have a dark, sad mother,
Whose bosom is bare to view;
So they haste, in their springtide beauty,
To clothe her worn heart anew.

They perish; but she endureth,
To faint in the Winter's scorn,
With a life-warmth buried within her
Through which other Springs are born.

As the shadows dance hither and thither,
The gleams of thy consciousness pass,
As a lamp wakes its fitful glimmer
In the heart of a sleeping glass.
The shrouded ghost of the future
Stands near, while I hold thee fast;
And the traits of my race turn slowly
My thoughts to the long-linked past.

O Future! what sorrows gather
In the folds of thy hanging veil?
O Past, shalt thou flower further
In passions comprest and pale?
O thou who art past and future,
Thou Present of life and soul!
We lift our sad eyes to thy features,
Our thoughts to thy great control.

Thy manhood lies crouching within thee,
For the leap of its coming years;
Thy heart takes its long vibration
From the mother's fountain of tears;
The helpful things and the hurtful
Weave round thee their waiting spell:
Oh! look to the God that commands them,
And all shall be suffered well.

THE UNWELCOME MESSAGE.

A DISMAL Postman passes by, —
    I fear his sullen knock :
'Twill strike a shiver through the door,
    And paralyze the lock.

"Plague not this unoffending house ;
    It owes no shameful debt ;
Nor guilty chamber doth it hide
    Where evil guests are met.

Here gentle heart and gentle blood
    Their life-surroundings bless ;
And days glide by with happy toil,
    And measured thankfulness.

The messengers who enter here
    Are glad and bright of eye,
Freighted with precious words that stir
    Responsive minstrelsy."

" The note is brief, the seal is sharp,
    The characters are pale :
I cannot err in their address ;
    My letters never fail.

If you the door will not unbar,
    The window answers well,
Less lofty than the turret where
    I touch the passing bell.

When you have read, the feast may speed,
    The business, as you list :
But, somehow, where my foot has stept,
    The joy of joys is missed ;

And on the heart of working week
  A Sabbath falls of rest,
Unwished ; yet He who sends me here
  Declares his errand blest."

MY CRUCIFIX.

BABY sweet is dying, — he is dying.
Place the crucifix above his head;
It conveys a sympathetic sighing,
Tears of kindred with the tears we shed.

For no succor from this head anointed
Do I bring its sorrow near his pain:
Death must come where dying is appointed;
But this dead one saith, "I live again."

Well I deem some virtue must be hidden
In the hero heart that would not die:
By those firm lips, Baby shall be bidden
To take hope, and live immortally.

A WINTER THOUGHT.

The flower of my love is sleeping,
Locked in his icy funeral mound :
The Frost, stern sentinel, is keeping
Earth's trancèd blossoms under ground.

The Spring shall bring the sweet appearing
Of buds, her radiant breath shall free ;
But my heart blossom, most endearing,
Shall rest, a flower of Memory.

A sterner sentinel is waiting
Our ban of severance to remove :
Death must resolve our separation,
Chill Herald of the Spring of Love.

SPRING-BLOSSOMS.

THE little daisies, two by two,
The lilies wet with frosted dew,
The sweet procession of the Spring
Carries my baby's offering.

I leave the thoughts that take his place,
Imaginations winged in space,
And fold his shadow to my breast,
With the dear lips that mine have prest.

Ever my introverted eyes
Recover that past paradise ;
Not without hell pain shuddered through
Where life declined, to rise anew.

Oh! to my darling carry this,
The old-time phrase, the frequent kiss;
Remind him how, in his decay,
My life's enamel melts away.

Tell him my time must also come
To enter his restricted home,
Where my soul furniture shall be
His lovely immortality.

REMEMBRANCE.

THERE was a time when thy dear face to me
Was but a dream, with nameless pangs between.
Three happy years upheld the fatal screen
Whose fall left blank and bitterness for thee.

As one who at a gracious drama sits,
And builds long vistas in its magic ways,
" For this must come, and this ;" and while he stays
The end consigns him to the silent streets :

So did I stand when thy sweet play was done,
Wondering what spell the curtain still should hide,
Waiting and weeping, till my saintly guide
Took by the hand, and pitying said, " Pass on."

So thou art hid again, and wilt not come
For any knocking at the veilèd door ;
Nor mother-pangs, nor nature, can restore
The heart's delight and blossom of thy home.

And I with others, in the outer court,
Must sadly follow the excluding will,
In painful admiration of the skill
Of God, who speaks his sweetest sentence short.

LITTLE ONE.

My dearest boy, my sweetest!
For paradise the meetest;
The child that never grieves me,
The love that never leaves me;
The lamb by Jèsu tended;
The shadow, star befriended;
In Winter's woe and straining,
The blossom still remaining.

Days must not find me sitting
Where shadows dim are flitting
Across the grassy measure
That hides my buried treasure,
Nor bent with tears and sighing,
More prone than thy down-lying:

I have a freight to carry,
A goal, — I must not tarry.

If men would garlands give me,
If steadfast hearts receive me,
Their homage I'd surrender
For one embrace most tender;
One kiss, with sorrow in it,
To hold thee but one minute,
One word, our tie recalling,
Beyond the gulf appalling.

Since God's device doth take thee,
My fretting should forsake thee;
For many a mother borrows
Her comfort from the sorrows
Her vanished darling misses,
Transferred to heavenly blisses.
But I must ever miss thee,
Must ever call and kiss thee,
With thy sweet phantom near me,
And only God to hear me.

The pomp with which I mourn thee,
I who have proudly borne thee,
Is not of weary sables,
Nor unsubstantial fables;
While thou, in white apparel,
And crowned, above my laurel,
Passest from my discerning
To more transcendent learning.

When thou wert taken from me,
Did better art become me,
And painful satisfaction
Wrung from some noblest action.
I mourn in simpler praying,
More work and less delaying,
In hope enforced that mellows
The crudeness of thy fellows,
Who, past thy lovely season,
Attempt the wars of Reason;
I mourn thee with endeavor
That loves and grieves forever.

CHOPIN.

WE saw him in the death-nest laid;
His wings were folded, sad and still;
The glowing tropic of his breast
Endured no more Life's winter chill.

But now, through Fancy's clouded gate,
He walks with Nature's spirit-kings;
The sceptre in his palsied hands
Strikes rapture at her deepest springs.

His life was like an opal gem
That breaks in many a painful thrill:
The risen rainbow of his soul
The heaven of song is spanning still;

While happy Love and Grief sublime
Unite their emblems on his brow,
And pave with zeal his shadowy court, —
A Lover once, a Master now.

HAMLET AT THE BOSTON.

WE sit before the row of evening lamps,
    Each in his chair,
Forgetful of November dews and damps,
    And wintry air.

A little gulf of music intervenes,
    A bridge of sighs,
Where still the cunning of the curtain screens
    Art's paradise.

My thought transcends these viols' shrill delight,
    The booming bass,
And, towards the regions we shall view to-night,
    Makes hurried pace.

The painted castle, and the unneeded guard
  That ready stand ;
The harmless Ghost, that walks with helm unbarred
  And beckoning hand.

And beautiful as dreams of maidenhood,
  That doubt defy,
Young Hamlet, with his forehead grief-subdued,
  And visioning eye.

O fair dead world, that from thy grave awak'st.
  A little while,
And in our heart strange revolution mak'st
  With thy brief smile !

O beauties vanished, fair lips magical,
  Heroic braves !
O mighty hearts, that held the world in thrall !
  Come from your graves !

The poet sees you through a mist of tears, —
    Such depths divide
Him, with the love and passion of his years,
    From you, inside!

The poet's heart attends your buskined feet,
    Your lofty strains,
Till earth's rude touch dissolves that madness sweet,
    And life remains:

Life that is something while the senses heed
    The spirit's call;
Life that is nothing when our grosser need
    Ingulfs it all.

And thou, young hero of this mimic scene,
    In whose high breast
A genius greater than thy life hath been
    Strangely comprest!

Wear'st thou those glories draped about thy soul
    Thou dost present?
And art thou by their feeling and control
    Thus eloquent?

'Tis with no feignèd power thou bind'st our sense,
    No shallow art;
Sure, lavish Nature gave thee heritance
    Of Hamlet's heart!

Thou dost control our fancies with a might
    So wild, so fond,
We quarrel, passed thy circle of delight,
    With things beyond;

Returning to the pillows rough with care,
    And vulgar food,
Sad from the breath of that diviner air,
    That loftier mood.

And there we leave thee, in thy misty tent
    Watching alone ;
While foes about thee gather imminent,
    To us scarce known.

Oh, when the lights are quenched, the music hushed,
    The plaudits still,
Heaven keep the fountain, whence the fair stream gushed,
    From choking ill !

Let Shakspeare's soul, that wins the world from wrong,
    For thee avail,
And not one holy maxim of his song
    Before thee fail !

So get thee to thy couch as unreproved
    As heroes blest ;
And all good angels, trusted in and loved,
    Attend thy rest !

IN MY VALLEY

From the hurried city fleeing,
From the dusty men and ways,
In my golden sheltered valley,
Count I yet some sunny days.

Golden, for the ripened Autumn
Kindles there its yellow blaze;
And the fiery sunshine haunts it
Like a ghost of summer days.

Walking where the running water
Twines its silvery caprice,
Treading soft the leaf-spread carpet,
I encounter thoughts like these: —

"Keep but heart, and healthful courage,
Keep the ship against the sea,
Thou shalt pass the dangerous quicksands
That insnare Futurity;

Thou shalt live for song and story,
For the service of the pen;
Shalt survive till children's children
Bring thee mother-joys again.

Thou hast many years to gather;
And these falling years shall bring
The benignant fruits of Autumn,
Answering to the hopes of Spring.

Passing where the shades that darkened
Grow transfigured to thy mind,
Thou shalt go with soul untroubled
To the mysteries behind;

Pass unmoved the silent portal
Where beatitude begins,
With an equal balance bearing
Thy misfortunes and thy sins."

Treading soft the leaf-spread carpet,
Thus the Spirits talked with me ;
And I left my valley, musing
On their gracious prophecy.

To my fiery youth's ambition
Such a boon were scarcely dear :
" Thou shalt live to be a grandame,
Work and die, devoid of fear."

" Now, as utmost grace it steads me,
Add but this thereto," I said :
" On the Matron's time-worn mantle
Let the Poet's wreath be laid."

ENDEAVOR.

"WHAT hast thou for thy scattered seed,
　　O Sower of the plain?
Where are the many gathered sheaves
　　Thy hope should bring again?"
"The only record of my work
　　Lies in the buried grain."

"O Conqueror of a thousand fields!
　　In dinted armor dight,
What growths of purple amaranth
　　Shall crown thy brow of might?"
"Only the blossom of my life
　　Flung widely in the fight."

"What is the harvest of thy saints,
　　O God! who dost abide?
Where grow the garlands of thy chiefs
　　In blood and sorrow dyed?
What have thy servants for their pains?"
　　"This only, — to have tried."

MEDITATION.

I.

WHETHER the aim I keep is right,
So far removed from sense and sight,
While half the goods that mortals prize
Lie hidden from my dream-bound eyes,
And others watch with subtler skill
To please the toy-bent human will?

For this one passions with her glance;
And this one weaves her swift romance;
And this in steadfast marble leaves
The passing bloom the moment gives;
And this one mints the golden coin,
Attendant on each glad design,
And in her state well pleased doth ride
Through streets that saw the Tarquin's pride;

While I plod cheerless after thee,
Thou unattained Philosophy.

For me no crowd admiring waits,
Nor lettered venture tempts the Fates,
Nor hangs my work on princely walls,
Nor title proud my merit calls,
Nor I and marble shall be wed
Except above my funeral bed.
Only my diagrams I know ;
And even these make greater show
Than thou, O mistress ! dost allow,
Pent inward by a silent vow.

But this I boast, — a simpler need,
That leaves untrammelled time to read
The sentence of a loftier book
Than aught that Gain and Rumor brook ;
The thrifty urging of the morn
That waits on nations newly born,
Bestowing promise more divine
Than checkered gold at day's decline ;

Faith that permits and passes growth,
Embracing God and Nature both.

The rainbow helps us from the storm;
But skies serene are uniform.
Though colored gems be fair, the white
Doth keep the undivided light.
The garden shows its radiant prism,
The lily hides her golden chrism,
And Truth and Peace are goods sincere
That fix the source of comforts near.

MEDITATION.

II.

SUBLIME and poor the bards of old
Their heavenly message heard and told,
Sequestered from the human crowd,
Who heed but warnings large and loud.

Nor velvet robe the prophet had,
In homely garments bound and clad ;
Nor dainty table gave them seat
Who with the gods might take their meat.

But Jesus poorest was of all :
Tended with oxen in the stall ;
From narrow bounds of household rule
Devising his immortal school ;

While mother's toil and father's thrift
His weighty problems did uplift ;
And this one's work, and that one's wine,
Were moulded into types divine.
The needy fishers were his friends,
Unlearned companions in his ends ;
And stripe, and shame, and felon tree
Aided his deathless victory.

So, Soul, be steadfast in thy lot,
In marble shade or rustic cot :
Permit the wealth the Fates bestow,
But in its void no pining know.

The richest human treasury,
The mine of thought, to all is free.
Let Pleasure mix her shallow drink
While twines Desert the iron link
Whose firmness, over time and space,
Transmits the virtue of the race.

Though fortunes fail, and prospects frown,
May Duty keep her matchless crown,
Nor Desolation bid depart
The glories of a guileless heart.

THE HOUSE OF REST.

I WILL build a house of rest,
Square the corners every one:
At each angle on his breast
Shall a cherub take the sun;
Rising, risen, sinking, down,
Weaving day's unequal crown.

In the chambers, light as air,
Shall responsive footsteps fall:
Brother, sister, art thou there?
Hush! we need not jar nor call;
Need not turn to seek the face
Shut in rapture's hiding-place.

Heavy load and mocking care
Shall from back and bosom part ;
Thought shall reach the thrill of prayer,
Patience plan the dome of art.
None shall praise or merit claim,
Not a joy be called by name.

With a free, unmeasured tread
Shall we pace the cloisters through :
Rest, enfranchised, like the Dead ;
Rest till Love be born anew.
Weary Thought shall take his time,
Free of task-work, loosed from rhyme.

No reproof shall grieve or chill ;
Every sin doth stand confest ;
None need murmur, " This was ill : "
Therefore do they grant us rest ;
Contemplation making whole
Every ruin of the soul.

Pictures shall as softly look
As in distance shows delight ;
Slowly shall each saintly book
Turn its pages in our sight ;
Not the study's wealth confuse,
Urging zeal to pale abuse.

Children through the windows peep,
Not reproachful, though our own ;
Hushed the parent passion deep,
And the household's eager tone.
One above, divine and true,
Makes us children like to you.

Measured bread shall build us up
At the hospitable board ;
In Contentment's golden cup
Is the guileless liquor poured.
May the beggar pledge the king
In that spirit gathering.

Oh! my house is far away;
Yet it sometimes shuts me in.
Imperfection mars each day
While the perfect works begin.
In the house of labor best
Can I build the house of rest.

A VISIT TO C. H.

Let us sit with you, sister, before the low fire,
The scanty rag-carpet sufficing our feet:
You cannot command, and we need not require,
The window well shaded and soft-cushioned seat.

The children of pride scarcely come to your door,
And we who have entered walk not in their ways;
But experience brings to the rich and the poor
One value abiding in life's changeful days.

You are homely in breeding? Some one of your race
Had a spark of high blood, to immortals akin:
You are loath to be seen in this desolate place?
What honor may lack where the Muse is within?

A presence I feel in the God-lightened air,
The spell of the art I have followed so long:
In your calico garment and rough-twisted hair
Let us speak of your queendom, poor sister of song.

For, well may we know it, the tap that you hear,
When you lay down the needle, and take up the pen,
Is the summons august that the highest revere,
The greatest that visits the children of men.

The fountain of song in your bosom arose
When the small baby pillow was tenantless left?
You share with all mortals life's burthen of woes;
But all have not music, when grieved and bereft.

You dream o er the wash-tub, strive vainly to fix
Your thought on the small household matter in hand?
Some spices, no doubt, in your condiments mix,
Some flavors your neighbors can scarcely command.

The world is so hard, and the world is so cold?
And the dear-bought deliverance comes scanty and
    slow?
Say, whether is better, — its frosts to behold,
Or to share its heart winter, and shed no more glow?

I have found a rich blossom astray on the heath;
In sordid surroundings, an altar of love;
Or lashed in a cart, beyond beauty and breath,
The steed that should carry the bidding of Jove.

The town that hums near us has rich folk, besure, —
Its man of the Congress, its Mayor with his state,
Its lords of the spindle who pillage the poor,
Its pampered young people who quarrel and mate.

But not for their scanning I come here to-day;
The rich and the proud are forever the same:
My feet, poet sister, have found out this way,
Unsought and unsummoned, your kinship to claim.

A LEAF FROM THE BRYANT CHAPLET.

FRIENDS who greet the crownèd Poet, who detain the
    passing year
With the love that knows no passing, I attend your
    summons here.
Had ye suffered me in silence, I had thanked your
    courteous grace;
Happier yet, in rites so cordial, to have utterance and
    place.

In your city rows palatial has a mansion stood apart,
Not in aspect nor pretension, single in its saintly
    heart:
When the tides of greed and traffic swept the limits
    of the town,
'Twas a citadel of virtue, and a shrine of pure renown.

There the Muse that knew Anacreon, that made Roman
Horace great,
Shunning Cæsar's jewelled favors, at the modest fireside sate,
Lit the wintry coals with splendor, turned the deep historic page,
Held the burning lamp of Fancy to the problems of the age.

When the great ideas came singly to the crowded market-place,
Looking wanly for a welcome in each money-getting face,
And the high police of fashion urged the vagrants to give room,
They, our Chief of song encountering, grew speedily at home.

He had many a measure for us: at his forge he wrought twofold,
On the iron shield of Freedom, and the poet's links of gold.

All the while a song was singing, others better knew
than he;
For the even stanzas of his life made subtlest
melody.

He was a veteran leader ere his forehead gained its
snows;
And still before the pilgrim flock his silver summons
goes.
No wild and desert waste he brings, with lurid day
and night,
But pastures of serenity, and founts of clear delight.

We have journeyed far to praise him; let us also praise
the hour
For the travail throes of Conscience, and the newest
birth of power;
Let us praise the faultless victims, and the living, who
have bent
O'er the wealth of nature ravished, with a terrible
consent.

For Sorrow from the city to the martial camp has fled,
To hunt, with her funereal torch, the features of the
    dead.
Another and another son the sheaf of Fate doth bind,
But nothing of the thoughts of God, or hope of human
    kind.

Resurrection in the valley! resurrection on the shore!
When great Justice is established, we shall have our
    own once more;
Not like us, unfixed, inconstant in our issues great and
    small,
But a phalanx set in marble for the future's judgment
    call.

Long remain the noble Poet, priceless hostage of our
    love!
Vainly floats the wingèd message from the banquet
    halls of Jove,
Vainly voices from Valhalla name the champion of the
    free:
He has pæans yet to utter, he must crown our victory.

When the moment comes to claim him that must come
   to claim us all,
Hearts that cherish human longings will be darkened
   by his fall;
But immortal Truth shall welcome her adorer to her
   breast,
Saying, "Things are changed between us now. On
   earth I was thy guest."

HENRY WILSON'S SILVER WEDDING.

THE ancients had an age of gold,
  To silver thence descending,
While yet in baser metal told
  The series had its ending.

The golden time bore men divine;
  The silver, men heroic;
The brazen did to deeds decline,
  Rebuked of sage and stoic.

The mystic trine by Plato cast
  Was thus reversed from Nature:
The gold was in the unknown Past,
  Not in the unknown Future.

Our country knows the age of brass,
    Whose wary politician
Digs in that ore the steps that pass
    To recognized position.

But WILSON, from the lowlier base
    The silver vantage gaining,
Climbs ever towards the golden grace,
    With labor uncomplaining.

Well may the country thrive like him
    To whom her heart's beholden, —
His Present's Silver never dim,
    His Future always Golden!

THE NEW EXODUS.

"FORSAKE this flowery garden!" the frowning Angel
    said;
" Its vines no more may feed thee, compel from stones
    thy bread ;
Pursue the veins deep buried that hide thy wine and
    oil ;
Fruit shalt thou find with sorrow, and children rear in
    toil."

Oh! not in heathen vengeance the winged apostle
    spoke ;
Nor savage retribution the blooming fetters broke.
Man had an arm for labor, a strength to conquer
    pain,
A brain to plot and study, a will to serve and reign.

That will with slow arraying confronts itself with fate,
The pair unconscious twining the arches of the State.
Earth keeps her fairest garlands to crown the tireless spade ;
The fields are white with harvest, the hireling's fee is paid.

From tented field to city, to palace, and to throne,
Man builds with work his kingdom, and makes the world his own.
All welded with conditions is empire's golden ring :
The king must keep the peasant, the peasant feed the king.

The word of God once spoken, from truth is never lost ;
The high command once given, earth guards with jealous cost.
By this perplexing lesson, men build their busy schemes :
" The way of comfort lies not, kind Eden, through thy dreams."

I see a land before me, where manhood in its pride
Forgot the solemn sentence, the wage of toil denied :
" To wealth and lofty station some royal road must be ;
Our brother, bound and plundered, shall earn us
    luxury.

One half of knowledge give him for service and for
    skill,
The nobler half withholding, that moulds the manly
    will :
From justice bar his pleadings, from mercy keep his
    prayers ;
His daughters for our pleasure, his sons to serve our
    heirs."

Again the frowning Angel commandeth to depart,
With fiery scourge of terror, with want and woe of
    heart :
" Go forth ! the earth is weary to bear unrighteous
    feet ;
Release your false possession ; go, work that ye may
    eat.

Bring here the light of knowledge, the scale of equal
    rule ;
Bring the Republic's weapons, the forum and the
    school :
The Dagon of your worship is broken on his shrine ;
The palm of Christian mercy brings in the true divine."

So from your southern Eden the flaming sword doth
    drive ;
Your lesson is appointed ; go, learn how workmen
    thrive !
Not sloth has fee of plenty, nor pride of stately crest ;
But thou of God beloved, O Labor crowned with
    rest !

PARRICIDE.

O'ER the warrior gauntlet grim
Late the silken glove we drew,
Bade the watch-fires slacken dim
In the dawn's auspicious hue.
 Staid the armèd heel ;
 Still the clanging steel ;
Joys unwonted thrilled the silence through.

Glad drew near the Easter tide ;
And the thoughts of men anew
Turned to Him who spotless died
For the peace that none shall rue.
 Out of mortal pain
 This abiding strain
Issued : " Peace, my peace, I give to you."

Musing o'er the silent strings,
By their apathy opprest,
Waiting for the spirit-wings,
To be touched and soul-possessed,
 "I am dull," I said:
 " Treason is not dead ;
Still in ambush lurks that shivering guest."

Then a woman's shriek of fear
Smote us in its arrowy flight ;
And a wonder wild and drear
Did the hearts of men unite.
 Has the seed of crime
 Reached its flowering-time,
That it shoots to this audacious height?

Then, as frosts the landscape change,
Stiffening from the summer's glow,
Grew the jocund faces strange,
Lay the loftiest emblem low :
 Kings are of the past,
 Suffered still to last ;
These twin crowns the present did bestow.

Fair assassin, murder white,
With thy serpent speed avoid
Each unsullied household light,
Every conscience unalloyed.
    Neither heart nor home
    Where good angels come
Suffer thee in nearness to abide.

Slanderer of the gracious brow,
The untiring blood of youth,
Servant of an evil vow,
Of a crime that beggars ruth,
    Treason was thy dam,
    Wolfling, when the Lamb,
The Anointed, met thy venomed tooth.

With the righteous did he fall,
With the sainted doth he lie :
While the gibbet's vultures call
Thee, that, 'twixt the earth and sky,
    Disavowed of both
    In their Godward troth,
Thou mayst make thy poor amend, and die.

If it were my latest breath,
Doomed his bloody end to share,
I would brand thee with his death
As a deed beyond despair.
 Since the Christ was lost
 For a felon's cost,
None like thee of vengeance should beware.

Leave the murderer, noble song,
Helpless in the toils of fate :
To the just thy meeds belong,
To the martyr, to the state.
 When the storm beats loud
 Over sail and shroud,
Tunefully the seaman cheers his mate.

Never tempest lashed the wave
But to leave it fresher calm ;
Never weapon scarred the brave
But their blood did purchase balm.
 God hath writ on high
 Such a victory
As uplifts the nation with its psalm.

Honor to the heart of love,
Honor to the peaceful will,
Slow to threaten, strong to move,
Swift to render good for ill!
 Glory crowns his end,
 And the captive's friend
From his ashes makes us freemen still.

PARDON.

PAINS the sharp sentence the heart in whose wrath it
    was uttered,
        Now thou art cold;
· Vengeance, the headlong, and Justice, with purpose
    close muttered,
        Loosen their hold.

Death brings atonement; he did that whereof ye accuse
    him, —
        Murder accurst;
But, from that crisis of crime in which Satan did lose
    him,
        Suffered the worst.

Harshly the red dawn arose on a deed of his doing,
        Never to mend;
But harsher days he wore out in the bitter pursuing
        And the wild end.

So lift the pale flag of truce, wrap those mysteries
round him,
In whose avail
Madness that moved, and the swift retribution that
found him,
Falter and fail.

So the soft purples that quiet the heavens with
mourning,
Willing to fall,
Lend him one fold, his illustrious victim adorning
· With wider pall.

Back to the cross, where the Saviour uplifted in dying
Bade all souls live.
Turns the reft bosom of Nature, his mother, low
sighing,
Greatest, forgive!

WELCOME.

They are coming, O our brothers! they are coming;
From the formless distance creeps the growing sound,
Like a rill-fed torrent, in whose rapid summing
Stream doth follow stream, till waves of joy abound.

These have languished in the shadow of the prison,
Long with hunger pains and bitter fever low:
Welcome back our lost, from living graves arisen,
From the wild despite and malice of the foe.

These have heard the cannon roar, the musket rattle;
Where grim death affronted, these have flown before:
Set their standards in the fiery tide of battle
Till the red waves parted, and the right went o'er.

As the Genii of the clouds refresh with water
Plants and precious seeds that bear the life of States,
These have poured their blood in meadows sown with
    slaughter,
Where the harvest of the Land's redemption waits.

Haste, ye mothers! let your household vigils slacken;
In your glad attire arrayed, go banded forth:
For these martial men, these ranks the sun doth
    blacken,
Are your babes indeed, the jewels of the North.

By the loves ye prize and live for, ask that never
Need so sore again the heart of home invade:
Neither brazen trump, nor wires that wail and quiver,
Bid you yield the living, and take back the dead.

Better let them build who rear the house of nations
Than that Fate should rock it to foundation stone:
Leave the earth her storms, the stars their perturba-
    tions,
Steadfast welfare stays where Justice binds her zone.

When the human faults that mix in human labor
Miss the measure set to caution and constrain,
Let the wise of heart instruct his ruder neighbor,
Let the loving soul hold violence in chain.

But when Falsehood lifts her challenge cry stupendous,
When the fiery angel bars our gates of bliss,
Ask the holy heavens such hosts again to lend us,
With such leaders, such a righteous cause as this.

THE END.

www.ingramcontent.com/pod-product-compliance
Lightning Source LLC
Chambersburg PA
CBHW030736230426
43667CB00007B/734